CONSTRUCTING AND DECONSTRUCTING WOMAN'S POWER

Edited by

Beth J. Seelig

Robert A. Paul

Carol B. Levy

KARNAC

LONDON NEW YORK

First published in 2002 by
H. Karnac (Books) Ltd.
6 Pembroke Buildings, London NW10 6RE

A subsidiary of Other Press LLC, New York

Cartoon on p. 76 by Marji Smith, from the Donna Quixote series published in NMWA magazine.

Cartoon on p. 77 by Bill Griffith. Reprinted with special permission of King Features Syndicate.

British Library Cataloguing in Publication Data

A C.I.P. for this book is available from the British Library

ISBN 1 85575 291 3

10 9 8 7 6 5 4 3 2 1

Edited, designed, and produced by Communication Crafts

Printed in Great Britain

www.karnacbooks.com

CONTENTS

THE NAVEL
Maternal power

THE WOMB
Creative power

THE PHALLUS
Point/counterpoint

PREFACE

Constructing and Deconstructing Woman's Power is a selection of papers presented at the interdisciplinary conference, "Women and Power—Psychoanalytic Perspectives on Women in Relationships, Groups and Hierarchies", jointly sponsored by the Committee on Women and Psychoanalysis (COWAP) of the International Psychoanalytical Association, the Emory University Psychoanalytic Institute, the Department of Psychiatry and Behavioral Sciences of the Emory School of Medicine, the Emory University Psychoanalytic Studies Program, and the Atlanta Foundation for Psychoanalysis, in conjunction with the American Psychoanalytic Association. The symposium took place at the Emory University Conference Center in Atlanta from 25 to 27 February 2000. It was the first of a series of conferences sponsored by COWAP in North America, with participants from North America, Latin America, Europe, and the Middle East.

Having entered a new millennium, there are pressing and complex challenges for us as individuals and as members of the global family. These challenges can foster new forms of creative interaction and growth. They can also lead to disagreement and dissension. Issues of power, conflict, and reconciliation are central to psychological well-being and social functioning.

Power and gender issues in particular can be dangerous and polarizing or exciting and enriching. The discipline of psychoanalysis has much to offer in exploration of these areas. Until recently, psychoanalysts have shied away from grappling with some of the knotty theoretical and conceptual issues arising from the social applications of power and gender. This has been changing recently both in the United States and internationally.

The editors of this volume hope that its publication will contribute to the understanding of power in women, elucidate the differences in power between the sexes, and generate and synthesize new approaches to some of the challenges posed by these differences.

ACKNOWLEDGEMENTS

This book was made possible by the hard work of a large number of contributors who made the "Women and Power" conference a success. We would like to thank the Office of the President of the University, Office of the Provost, Office of the Dean of the Graduate School, Office of the Dean of the Medical School, Chairman of the Department of Psychiatry and Behavioral Sciences, Emory Psychoanalytic Studies Program, Office of the Dean of Emory College, the Hightower Fund, the Emory Women's Studies Program in addition to the Atlanta Foundation for Psychoanalysis, and Eli Lilly and Company for the generous educational grants that made the conference possible.

There were far too many excellent papers presented in the "Women and Power" symposium to be included in this small volume. In addition to the authors whose essays appear in this book, we would like to thank the conference faculty whose papers could not be included in this book: Fahima Charafeddine, Susan F. Gantt, Otto F. Kernberg, Eleanor Maccoby, Robert Michels, Malkah Tolpin Notman, Ethel S. Person, Gail S. Reed, Arlene Kramer Richards, Steven P. Roose, Brenda Clorfene Solomon, Zachary N. Stowe, Phyllis Tyson, and Kim Wallen.

Many members of the faculty of the Emory Psychoanalytic Institute, the Department of Psychiatry and Behavioral Sciences, as well as psychiatry residents, and graduate students in the Emory Psychoanalytic Studies Program participated in planning the conference and chairing and coordinating individual sessions. We would like to thank Gail I. Anderson, Jason S. Breyan, Samuel B. Brown, Susan E. Chance, Brenda Crosby, Alice Dokter, Edward A. Gamarra, Sybil A. Ginsburg, R. Peery Grant, Sharon C. Grover, Wendy Jacobson, Salley S. Jessee, Jason B. Jones, Rose P. Jordan, Nadine Kaslow, Steven T. Levy, Phyllis B. Rosen, Lisa S. Rosof, Noha H. Sadek, Ann C. Schwartz, Julie Sexeny, and Jennifer L. Shaw.

We owe a special debt of gratitude to William M. Chace, President of Emory University, and to Rebecca S. Chopp, Provost and Executive Vice President of Academic Affairs, for supporting the concept of this endeavour and to Otto Kernberg, President of the International Psychoanalytical Association, for creating the Committee on Women and Psychoanalysis, where the idea originated for this international interdisciplinary meeting focusing on power, gender, conflict, and reconciliation.

ABOUT THE EDITORS AND CONTRIBUTORS

The editors

Carol B. Levy is a Senior Associate in the Department of Psychiatry at the Emory University School of Medicine and a candidate at the Florida Psychoanalytic Institute.

Robert A. Paul is currently the Interim Dean of Emory College. He is the Charles Howard Candler Professor of Anthropology and Interdisciplinary Studies at Emory and is also an Associate Professor in the Department of Psychiatry and Behavioral Sciences in the Emory School of Medicine. He is past President of the Society for Cultural Anthropology, the former Editor of *ETHOS: The Journal of the Society for Psychological Anthropology,* and the founding Director of Emory's Psychoanalytic Studies Program. A Training and Supervising Psychoanalyst at the Emory University Psychoanalytic Institute, he maintains a private practice in psychoanalysis.

Beth J. Seelig is Professor of Psychiatry and Behavioral Sciences, Emory University School of Medicine, and Director of and Training and Supervising Psychoanalyst at the Emory University Psychoanalytic Institute. She is North American Chair of the Committee on Women and Psychoanalysis (COWAP) of the International Psychoanalytical Association (IPA) and Chair of the Science Section of the American Psychoanalytic Association. She has presented widely and has published articles and chapters on psychoanalysis, psychotherapy, female development, altruism, masochism, and consultation in the course of psychoanalytic treatment.

The contributors

Alcira Mariam Alizade is a Psychiatrist and Training Analyst of the Argentine Psychoanalytic Association. She was Latin American co-chair of COWAP (1998–2001) and is current Chair of COWAP. She is author of *Feminine Sensuality* (1992), *Near Death: Clinical Psychoanalytical Studies* (1995), *Time for Women* (1996); *The Lone Woman* (1999), and *Positivity in Psychoanalysis* (2002).

Nancy J. Chodorow is Professor of Sociology and Clinical Professor of Psychology at the University of California at Berkeley and a faculty member of the San Francisco Psychoanalytic Institute and is in private practice in Oakland, California. Her books include the award-winning *The Reproduction of Mothering* (1999), *Feminism and Psychoanalytic Theory* (1989), *Femininities, Masculinities, Sexualities* (1994), and *The Power of Feelings* (1999, winner of the L. Bryce Boyer Prize). She is American Book Review Editor of the *International Journal of Psycho-Analysis* and Associate Editor of *Studies in Gender and Sexuality*. She is a recipient of the Distinguished Contribution to Women and Psychoanalysis Award of Section 5 of Division 39. Her most recent Fellowship was at the Radcliffe Institute for Advanced Study, Harvard (2001–2002).

Robert Alan Glick is Professor of Clinical Psychiatry, Columbia University, and Attending Psychiatrist, New York Presbyterian Hospital. He is Director of and Training and Supervising Psychoanalyst at the Columbia University Center for Psychoanalytic Training and Research. He has presented widely and has published on aspects of psychiatric education, psychiatric emergencies, psychoanalytic education, psychoanalytic identity, psychoanalytic affect theory, and masochism in major psychoanalytic and psychiatric journals and in book chapters, and he has edited five books.

Dorothy E. Holmes is Professor of Clinical Psychology, George Washington University, and Training and Supervising Analyst, Baltimore-Washington Institute for Psychoanalysis. She has published articles on the intrapsychic and transference–countertransference role of sex, race, and class in psychoanalytic treatment and the role of superego constraints on ego growth.

Elizabeth Lloyd Mayer is Associate Clinical Professor in the Psychology Department, University of California at Berkeley, and the Psychiatry Department, University of California Medical Center, San Francisco. She is Training and Supervising Psychoanalyst at the San Francisco Psychoanalytic Institute and a Fellow of the International Consciousness Research Laboratories at Princeton and is in private practice in Berkeley, California. Her forthcoming book, *Making Sense of the Extraordinary*, is due for release in 2003.

Helen Meyers is Clinical Professor of Psychiatry at Columbia University College of Physicians and Surgeons. She is Supervising and Training Psychoanalyst at and past Associate Director of the Columbia Psychoanalytic Center for Training and Research. She is Vice-President of the IPA and Past North American Chair of COWAP and is on the Steering Committee of the Committee on Psychoanalytic Education. She is on the editorial boards of major psychoanalytic journals. She is author of some 40 articles and chapters in books on various topics in psychoanalysis, including numerous works on female psychology, and has edited *Between Analyst and Patient: New Dimensions in Countertransference and Transference* (1986).

Joan Raphael-Leff is a practicing Psychoanalyst and Professor of Psychoanalysis at the Centre for Psychoanalytic Studies at the University of Essex. She is past Chair of COWAP (1998–2001). She has over 70 publications and 9 books, including *Psychological Processes of Childbearing* (1991), *Pregnancy—The Inside Story* (1993), *Female Experience—Three Generations of British Women Psycho-analysts on*

Work with Women (1997, co-edited with Rosine Jozef Perelberg), *Spilt Milk—Perinatal Loss and Breakdown* (2000), *Ethics of Psychoanalysis* (2000), *Between Sessions and Beyond the Couch* (2002), and *Parent- Infant Psychodynamics* (2002). Her past and present involvements include the Advisory Council for International Association for Relational Psychoanalysis and Psychotherapy, the Executive Committee of the Marce Society for Prevention of Puerperal Illness, the Royal Society of Medicine's Forum on the Newborn, and the Association of Infant Mental Health, U.K. She is an External Consultant to the Anna Freud Centre under-five's section, the Tavistock Clinic's Marital Studies Institute, PIPPINS, and various perinatal projects overseas.

Ellen Handler Spitz is Professor of Visual Arts in the Honors College and Graduate Faculty of the University of Maryland. She writes and lectures on psychoanalysis and the humanities. She is the author of *Art and Psyche* (1985), *Image and Insight* (1991), *Museums of the Mind* (1994), and *Inside Picture Books* (1999). She is also a former fellow of the Getty Center for the History of Art and the Humanities, the Radcliffe Institute for Advanced Study, and the Center for Advanced Study at Stanford University.

Miriam Tasini is Professor of Psychiatry at the Department of Psychiatry, University of California at Los Angeles Medical School, and Training and Supervising Psychoanalyst at Los Angeles Psychoanalytic Institute. Her interests and publications are in the area of mind–body relationships and teaching psychodynamic principles.

Elisabeth Young-Bruehl is on the faculty of the Columbia Center for Psychoanalytic Training and Research and is in private practice in New York City. She is the author of many books, including *Anna Freud: A Biography* (1988), *Creative Characters* (1991), *The Anatomy of Prejudices* (1996), and (with Faith Bethelard) *Cherishment: A Psychology of the Heart* (2000).

INTRODUCTION

The title of the conference, "Women and Power", on which this book is based brings together two words often regarded as antithetical, at least consciously and in interpersonal discourse. Indeed, this antithesis is often exaggerated defensively. Changes in social and intellectual contexts have made it more common and comfortable to consider issues of gender, power, and women's issues as complex interwoven constructions.

What is a woman, and what is power? Neither question can be answered simply. Our internal images of women and power are conscious and unconscious constructions to which biology, fantasy, prejudice, and anxiety all contribute. Our authors address the relevant considerations from a variety of psychoanalytic as well as social, cultural, and philosophical perspectives.

The space

Our first three authors examine externally imposed and self-imposed limitations on the acquisition of power by women. Commonly referred to as the glass ceiling and sometimes amended to include concrete walls or sticky floors, these constructs provide the metaphorical space in which to explore the complex and multifaceted nature of impediments to women's ascent in organizational hierarchies in general and the workplace in particular. Dorothy E. Holmes sees the societal and especially the parental proscription against the expression of aggression in girls as the basis for adult conflicts about success in women. She believes that the origins of an internal glass ceiling are manifest early in development and interfere with the acquisition of secondary-process aptitudes necessary for the management of aggression. In an illustrative analytic case, Holmes points to the total transference situation, rather than the analysand's verbal productions, as the likely place for therapeutic interventions.

Nancy J. Chodorow examines the metaphor of the glass ceiling and related notions. She argues for a more complex and inclusive consideration of diverse factors that create the glass ceiling. These include internal and external limitations, explicit and implicit biases, sociocultural expectations, family dynamics, and manifestations of intrapsychic and interpersonal conflict and compromise. In three clinical vignettes, Chodorow illustrates the complexities of inner and outer inhibitions that interfere with women's achievement and enjoyment of success.

Miriam Tasini discusses work inhibition in women, citing the roles of identification and inhibition of aggression in creating an internal glass ceiling. She builds her arguments around two related issues. First, she emphasizes that women, more regularly than men, confuse hostile and non-hostile aggression and treat their competitive and assertive stirrings as hostile. Tasini then points to the mitigating influence of benign positive identifications with successful women and men (mainly parents). These identifications allow some women to consolidate separate representations of hostile and non-hostile aggression, permitting competition, assertion, and success without guilt, feelings of unlovableness, or fear of rivalrous retribution. Her four clinical vignettes illustrate varying identifications and their consequences.

The navel

Despite the familiar stereotypes of powerlessness in women, most people recognize in the act of childbirth an extraordinary and awesome power. This specifically female power involves both the creation of life and the very complex and personal ongoing power of mothering. Joan Raphael-Leff and Ellen Handler Spitz address the unique components of maternal power in the section entitled "The Navel". Raphael-Leff outlines the growing trend among contemporary mothers to experience motherhood in isolation, thereby increasing their power over their children but also exacerbating their vulnerability to the inevitable burdens of the mothering role. She explores maternal ambivalence and the consequences of defensive avoidance of maternal hatred and also addresses the intersubjective psychological structuring between mother and baby. Finally, Raphael-Leff discusses the complex somatic and psychic sources of conflict and emphasizes transgenerational effects.

Spitz describes the individuation of adolescent girls, with particular attention to mother–daughter conflicts viewed from an object relations perspective. She uses a film, *A World Apart,* to illustrate what occurs when powerful sociopolitical pressures are added to the already intense separation–individuation issues of female adolescence. She highlights the salient developmental difficulties of the mother–daughter pair portrayed in the film. Themes of maternal unavailability, empathic failure, good/bad object splits, and disempowerment of women are highlighted and related to transgenerational, political, and moral dilemmas. These are portrayed in a powerful film that serves as the backdrop for Spitz's study of conflicted mothering.

The womb

The power that women possess both to create life and to influence the development of others also finds expression in creative venues outside the sphere of actual biological maternity. The section on women and creativity brings us out of the physicality of biological procreation into the symbolic womb in which creative expression is nurtured. Elizabeth Lloyd Mayer and Elisabeth Young-Bruehl innovatively approach the topic of feminine creativity, focusing on its development and potential for unique expression.

Mayer argues for the centrality of a radically expanded recognition of connectedness in relation to creativity and a new understanding of the universe. This is presented as an essentially feminine contribution, although not restricted to women. According to Mayer, living "on the margins" allows women a different observational perspective that can transform both how we learn to love and the tools psychoanalysis employs. Mayer sees boundaried conceptualizations giving way to new notions of connectedness, primarily a women's way of experiencing or ordering experience.

Young-Bruehl focuses on three conceptualizations of creativity, which she relates to adolescent identity consolidation. She describes these as character ideals, projections of endopsychic perceptions of adolescent creativity. These three ideals characterize creativity as stemming from the harnessing of creative forces by an omnipotent, overpowering authority; the artisanal figure who shapes, moulds, and forms a creative self; and the purifying ascetic who creates by stripping away to pure essentials. Young-Bruehl describes a group of creative women of the third type, whose creativity—purification is centred, at least in part, on gender conflicts.

The phallus

No book about women and their power could be complete without some consideration of the significance of the phallus as male organ and signifier of power and potency. However, this being a book about the construction and deconstruction of the power of *woman*, we deliberately limit the discourse related to male forms of power and disempowerment. We have chosen three papers that address men's relation to women and power and to power in women.

Our first contributor to this section, Alcira Mariam Alizade, centres on the psychological significance of the genital difference and the disparity in physical power between men and women. She regards an acceptance of castration as being fundamental to a specifically feminine form of power. For Alizade, feminine power is a benign force that can be an attribute of men as well as of women.

Robert Alan Glick describes the fear and awe men have of women, noting Freud's failures to recognize that fantasies of woman as inherently damaged human beings defends against awareness of the power that women have over men. Glick enumerates familiar ways men disparage women in order to obscure their own vulnerabilities, emphasizing male dependence on women as helping them overcome their own inadequacies. He also discusses the nature and forms of female power over men and describes clinical examples of men who are unable to develop enduring and gratifying relationships with women.

Our final author, Helen Meyers, tackles the issue of men's conscious and unconscious views of women and power as a woman analyst interfacing with male patients, colleagues, and friends and through her observations of the sociopolitical arena. First, she distinguishes between the notion of power in women, which she views as an internal sense of strength predicated on the ability to be self-assertive, and women in power, which is more externally observable and implies a more aggressive stance. Meyers discusses the significance of the developing male's preoedipal and oedipal wishes, jealousy and envy, and identifications with the mother in relation to his later views of power in women. She illustrates these unconscious and early developmental determinants in two clinical vignettes of male analysands. More consciously derived male views of women in power, as opposed to powerful women, are also described. Meyers ends by elaborating upon the various methods utilized by women to attain positions of power, including seduction and nurturance.

Psychoanalysts, by virtue of their emphasis on psychic reality, are in a position to elucidate the uniquely personal ways gender and power are experienced by women. These private experiences and modes of experiencing play a significant role in the success or failure of lives fashioned by individual women and are central determinants of their happiness and satisfaction. The psychoanalytic perspective presented in the book complements the sociocultural views that have become increasingly popular in recent years, particularly in the works of feminist authors. Considering the interplay between inner and outer realities and the adaptations to both permits a more complete and comprehensive understanding of human behaviour and experience. It is in this spirit that our psychoanalytic authors have explored the unconscious intra-psychic and interpersonal manifestations of power in women and their developmental, psychological, and relational origins and consequences.

THE SPACE
Ceilings, walls, and floors

CHAPTER ONE

"Glass ceilings": their origins, psychodynamic manifestations, and consequences in women

Dorothy E. Holmes

A psychodynamic formulation of "glass ceilings" faced by women

"She came, she conquered, she burned" (Hunter, 1999). This is a description of Joan of Arc written by a critic of the film, *The Messenger: The Story of Joan of Arc*. In this movie, Joan of Arc's life was so absurdly miscast as to render every strength of hers as silly or crazy. For example, her abundant and unshakeable faith was not considered as a sustaining asset in her personality but was assigned a crazy meaning—as the fuel for a revenge motive in response to having watched her sister being murdered and raped (in that order!) by an English knight. Hopefully, it is unnecessary to clarify that no credible history records that Joan or her sister suffered those particular traumas.

The pathologizing of women's ambitions and punishing women for pursuing their ambitions remain with us today, and not just in films. Social consciousness regarding women has been raised to the extent that the number of women represented in the professions is significantly higher than it was a quarter of a century ago. In medicine, for example, the numbers have quadrupled. Nevertheless, glass-ceiling effects remain entrenched. As a recent study pointed out, "There continues to be an invisible glass ceiling effect in medicine. There were only forty-seven women chairpersons of all clinical departments in U.S. medical schools, and in paediatrics, a field that attracts the largest number of women, there were only five [female] chairpersons in a total of 128 U.S. medical school paediatric departments in 1989" (Rimm, Rimm-Kaufman, & Rimm, 1999, pp. 323–324).

Psychoanalysts are not the only ones to recognize that the factors that govern these phenomena are elusive and deeply subjective. For example, Williams (2000), a law professor and family law advocate, wrote: "The practices that add up to the glass ceiling are often unconscious, as when women's work is scrutinized more closely than men's" (p. 69). She further noted that the qualities most often rewarded with high-level assignments and promotions—for example, being committed and serious—are perceived by high-level executives to be embodied in men more than women.

How do the limitations that are imposed on women by sexist attitudes and practices in our culture get internalized by them? Parens' work (1991) on the early development of aggression is instructive here. One of the subjects reported on in that infant observation study was a 3½-month-old baby girl whose behaviour was observed thus during feeding:

> Jane seemed to try to control the spoon mother put into her mouth, making quite vigorous efforts to feed herself. . . . Notable is the intense, work-like affect . . . the inner drivenness of that activity; . . . indeed, her entire body is involved in her effort. . . . [We found] affective behaviors suggestive of aggression which is neither hostile nor destructive prior to the structuring of the ego as an agency. [pp. 76–77]

Thus, aggression as goal-directed energy or ambition takes root in very early life, even before the ego is established as an agency—that is, when the mind is still primary-process-dominated. Furthermore, as Marcus (1999) pointed out about the early mind, it is "characterized by thing presentations [and] visual and somatosensory modes" (p. 849). Growth of ego agency is necessary for these trends to become optimally useful.

The necessary ego growth depends on developments in secondary-process capacity that are themselves dependent on what Marcus (1999) referred to as "environmental influence that we call experience or education" (p. 858).

It is my hypothesis that females in the course of development in our society will inevitably internalize the sexism aimed against the optimal, unconflicted uses of their aggression. As such, mobilization of their action potentials in pursuit of their goals will be more or less disturbed, and with varying degrees of severity, depending on how much, when, and in what kinds of ways their action tendencies are impeded over the course of development. Parens' work is pertinent here, too. He pointed out (1991) that in contrast to potential for non-hostile aggression which is inborn, the potential for hostile destructiveness is provoked in the self in response to an injury to self, or, one might say, to self-expression. Thus, the baby girl whose non-hostile aggression—let us say the first expressions of her ambition—is impeded has then to experience and manage hostile aggression.

"When you have your hand in the lion's mouth, pat the lion!"

Is it not highly likely that most girls learn over the course of development the dangers of directing their inborn, non-hostile aggression outward? Remember, "she came; she conquered; she burned." At this point I am also reminded of something my mother taught me to help me gain strategic, adaptive advantage in a competitive world.

During my formative years she recognized that our world was not welcoming of my advances as a female or as an African-American, and so she said: "When you have your hand in the lion's mouth, pat the lion." For women, often, the world of ambition and competition is the "lion's mouth". "Patting the lion" can be adaptive if it is for the purpose of removing oneself from danger. However, it is my view that society continues to define our world as a man's world and to demand that a woman's "place" (Janeway, 1971) is an assigned one of appeasement in relation to men in the work world. As such, I think that the ambitious girl growing to womanhood faces tremendous challenge in learning to acknowledge, accept, and adaptively use her own inborn non-hostile aggression. In a world such as ours where recognition and positive valuation of aggression is deemed the province of men, there is considerable pressure on females to cast their aggression out, to disavow and project it defensively. Thereby, they empty themselves of a necessary life force, and at times, in response to the inevitable injury to self when denied self-expression, they develop hostile aggression that may then be turned on the self and/or projected. Thus, the girl/woman ends up with a compound of potentials for hostile and non-hostile aggression and few incentives for learning to differentiate these urges and to gain conscious, masterly control over them.

In reviewing the available social-science literature on the problems of high-level professional women in our culture, I came upon a good illustration of the multiple forms and expressions of aggression in women. In Rimm's study of 1,000 successful professional women cited above (Rimm et al., 1999, pp. 311–312), among many other criteria for selection, only women who described themselves as happy in their work were selected as subjects. When responding to the various paper-and-pencil instruments of the study, by and large the subjects described themselves as being smart or talented and as having been intellectually gifted as children. However, of great interest to this chapter, these same women described that they felt a need to be true to their upbringings as "*good little girls*" (emphasis added) and, as such, not to brag. They then expressed surprise that they were considered successful enough to qualify for the study. A group of high-level female civil engineers, for example, when asked to participate in the study, hesitated on the grounds that they were not smart enough to be included in the study. Also, numerous subjects, including highly placed medical researchers, attributed career advancement and awards as much to serendipity and luck as to their smartness and persistence. I take these findings to illustrate that women make use of non-hostile aggression—that is, their ambition—to become successful. At the same time, they do not fully claim their success because they turn hostile aggression on themselves in the form of self-doubt and minimization of their accomplishments, and these are tendencies that are laid down in early childhood, or, as Parens' work informs us, in early infancy. As to the early roots of the tendency to use aggression to disparage oneself, the subjects of the study spoke of needing to limit their aggression early in their lives—that is, to be "good little girls". From a psychodynamic point of view, it is no surprise that the subjects then began to belittle themselves by attributing their very high achievement to factors beyond their control such as fate and serendipity.

Given the Rimm study results, we are obliged to understand further the intrapsychic representations and their consequences in women growing up under the influences of a society prejudiced against their achievement. Undoubtedly, these ambition-limiting prejudices are transmitted to females by society at large and through conflicted approval or disapproval of their ambitions by parents. In addition to knowing that these limiting influences are laid down in the mind, with the particular kinds of disturbances in the availability and uses of aggression I have outlined, we must press further to begin to try to understand the levels and kinds of psychic representation that these disturbances in aggression gain in the psychic organization of women. As reviewed earlier, Marcus (1999), in his study of the ego, pointed out that the necessary dominance of secondary process is a developmental process requiring favourable inputs from the environment through education and experience. Clearly, these channels will often not offer the female child the required "good-enough" experience to foster optimal secondary-process domination over her aggression. Again, consider the subjects who responded that they were happy in their work and began to detail various elements of their successfulness. Then, when they reminded themselves that they were brought up to be "good little girls", their answers showed signs of regression away from secondary-process domination. They began to attack and belittle themselves. The facile potential for such a regressive shift in women of such strong and high achievement is most noteworthy. I believe that the turning of hostile aggression on the self illustrated by the subjects in the Rimm study can represent two possibilities: for neurotically structured women, it may be a defence mechanism explainable in terms of the woman's neurosis; in addition, in some women—that is, those who have had early and chronic experiences in which non-hostile modes of aggression have been disallowed—I believe that their egos get battered with introjected hostile aggression which can result in an ego vulnerability or deficit. A later section, "Psychoanalytic Treatment of 'Glass-Ceiling' Effects", takes up these possibilities more explicitly: in the "It's Too Fine for Me" treatment report, I believe that the patient illustrated a co-mingling of neurotic aspects and ego weakness; in the vignette involving two women engaged in road rage, I think one can reasonably conjecture that ego weakness contributed to the shooting.

Memory systems and the internal registration of "glass ceilings" in women

So, when aggression in women is not secondary-process dominated, how might we begin to understand the psychic place and the vicissitudes women experience in the expression of their aggression? This question is important not only theoretically, but also in terms of therapeutic action to be considered in the context of a clinical vignette presented later in the chapter. I think that the emerging literature on declarative and procedural memory helps us answer the question. In a word, with declarative memory we gain access to events and information. It is sometimes referred to as autobiographical memory. It is well organized by age 5 years, and depends in large measure on development of the hippocampus. Procedural memory, on the other hand, is a system that, quoting Clyman (1991), organizes "The mental processes which culminate in an emotional state, as well as the consequences of that emotional state ... [and its] ... antecedents" (pp. 357–358). In contrast to declarative memory, procedural memory is thought to be organized at a subcortical level—specifically, in the basal ganglia, the cerebellum, and the amygdala.

As Fonagy has noted (1999): "Procedural memory is content-free, it is involved in acquiring sequences of actions, the 'HOW' of behaviour ... " (p. 216), and it "is evident earlier in development than declarative memory ..." (p. 217). There is laboratory evidence that strongly suggests that emotions and attitudes organized procedurally are extremely sturdy once established and are not subject to extinction. As I elaborated above, aggression is seeded deeply and early in the mind with inborn and acquired aspects. Given the restrictions imposed on the development and elaboration of aggression in girls, which are the focus of this chapter, is it not reasonable to conjecture that girls will harbour dimensions of their aggression in the procedural-memory system? That is, their aggression will be organized in what we can refer to as the "how to" system, in which they will learn the how to of becoming and lastingly being the "good little girl". Borrowing further from Marcus's review of ego psychology, it is of note that Freud provided us with our first approximations of knowledge about which the more recent research on memory informs us more exactly and fully.

Much of what today is classified in the procedural system Freud classified as primary process, including affect intensities. Lack of memory for same he classified as primary repression. He postulated that such experiences could not be recovered because they had never been associated with language. He did not, however, separate content (declarative memory) from contentless forms (procedural memory) and align each with its proper neuroanatomical structures. Jones (1993) did bring Freud's work forward in these regards and added to it substantially. Of particular interest here is her conceptualization of what she calls "postverbal infantile repression", which articulates a developmentally higher form of Freud's primary repression in which, "a linguistically competent child [i.e. one for whom there is verbal capacity to express an emotional state] . . . has no words [for the emotional state] . . . [because] no one has verbalized the experience for the child or help[ed] the child to verbalize it, [and] the experience may simply not be accessible later to verbal, or conscious, recall" (pp. 86–87). Jones developed this category to account for nonverbal encoding of affects and drive derivatives, as in primary repression, but with the difference that the encoding of these states occurs after the development of language. It may be that in the therapy situation with women, emotional states associated with damaged ambitions may be more readily accessible in the transference when the damage occurred postverbally versus preverbally, albeit that in both cases the encoding was nonverbal.

"Glass ceilings" and success neurosis in women

Before addressing clinical material proper, a brief summary of the modern success-neurosis literature is indicated. "Success neurosis" is a term that was articulated by Freud (1916d) to account for the urge to wreck one's success as punishment for oedipal guilt, and he acknowledged (1936a) the poverty of his youth as a factor that shaped his own success neurosis. Thus, relevant for this chapter, he proffered that real factors such as poverty can shape intrapsychic states and symptoms. Horney (1936) observed that severe resistances in treatment—that is, negative therapeutic reactions—are a manifestation of success neurosis. In linking success neurosis to negative therapeutic reactions, she was the first to raise the primacy of aggression and superego factors in the formation of success neurosis, thus going beyond Freud's association of aggression, superego, masochism, and negative therapeutic reaction. It was not until the 1960s, however, that preoedipal roots and symptomatic expressions of success neurosis were articulated. Frank (1977), in his study of success problems in graduate students, cited insufficiency of preoedipal parental love leading to profound depression. He also thought that the depression and its negative impact on success were sustained by a motive to punish the unloving parents. Szekely (1960) pointed out that preoedipally organized individuals might find success particularly threatening in that it requires them to mobilize improperly or incompletely neutralized drive derivatives. The possible clinical manifestations coming from such a fragile organization are elaborated in clear detail by Levy, Seelig, and Inderbitzin (1995), with particular focus on what happens clinically when there have been disturbances in the separation–individuation phase. Their material included patients who were trapped between an overly close relationship to one parent and the threatening envy of the other parent. Their clinical material illustrated that this constellation forces such patients into pathological narcissistic self-sufficiency in which promotions and successes are subject to disruption by grandiose excitement and manic exhibitionism.

I shall end this brief review of the success-neurosis literature with mention of Schafer's 1984 paper on the topic, for one of its foci is success neurosis in women. He recognized sexism as one of the determining factors in the development of success neurosis and the idealization of unhappiness as one of its expressions. He acknowledged that the experience of sexism across the life span is damaging to a woman's potentials for success, and he advised that psychoanalytic treatment be aimed at "[the] network of oral, anal, and phallic-exhibitionistic fantasies or fixations . . ." (p. 402) that lay beneath the damage.

Psychoanalytic treatment of "glass-ceiling" effects in women: the lion's mouth revisited

First, I draw your attention to the recent news story from Texas in which two working women were driving home from work in a routine, heavily congested rush hour. They repeatedly cut in front of each other in traffic. At a stopping point, one woman got out of her car and charged after the other one; the woman in the car reached for the gun on her passenger seat and shot the other one dead. This is a vivid example of how mobilization of aggression created unstable and regressive states in two women, with too easy accessibility in behaviour of hostile aggression and too little accessibility of purposeful non-hostile aggression. In a gripping public accounting of the shooting, the assailant had no idea why she shot the other woman. For me, this example expresses the pitfall for women of having been socialized to keep their hands in the lion's mouth. That is, women are taught to be wedded to the notion that aggression is inherently extremely dangerous and cannot be expressed by them, but, rather, that such expressions are the province of men. Here, external reality joins with whatever is dangerous about aggression in each female's fantasy life born of each woman's own unique intrapsychic makeup. The two reinforce prohibition against internal awareness of or outward expression of aggression. Keeping one's hand in the lion's mouth keeps the real and fantasied dangers located in the other. Sandler (1990) framed this eventuality thus: "Even if the presences in fantasy are persecuting, guilt-making ones, they nevertheless have the function of carrying the individual's own projected aggression, while at the same time providing a background feeling of safety. It is worth reminding ourselves here of the way in which battered children resist separation from their parents . . ." (p. 874). Such adaptations are brittle at best, as the showdown between the two Texan women shows. To the extent that society robs women of normal growth and development of aggression and denies them agency with respect to their aggression, a necessary component of psychic development is grossly distorted. Women are then left to ward off aggression and, thereby, have too little experience learning to master its various forms of containment and expression. Under duress, in the worst such cases, defences will not protect against murderous potential, as the story of the women in the Texas showdown illustrates.

My basic point is that the glass ceiling—that is, the societal proscriptions against expressions of aggression by women, with frustrations rather than rewards for ambition—adds a potentially devastating, crippling influence to whatever are the intrinsic normal-neurotic influences regarding their drives. Glass ceilings are laid down early in systems of the mind that are not readily retrieved. Women differ, of course, in the degree to which glass-ceiling effects damage them, but, whatever the degree, access to the damage is likely to be through transference manifestations of emotional states. Recovery of childhood wishes and goals may be a major therapeutic action for some women—specifically, those whose ambitions were affected less by glass ceilings and/or the effects occurred later in development and were repressed at the postverbal infantile level or beyond, using Jones's (1993) schema again. However, it seems likely to me that since sexism is so pervasive and the glass ceiling so thick and obdurate, some work at even earlier levels dominated by procedural memory will be necessary for many women. Those patients, as the news story example illustrates, have "emotional procedures and control structures which are inadequate to handle life's exigencies" (Clyman, 1991, p. 369). The best access to their difficulties is through how our patients are in the transference, to be contrasted with our usual emphasis on what they say. For example, even minute shifts in patients' emotional states, stereotypes in verbal and behavioural presentations, and the total interpersonal situation the patient creates in the transference with the analyst must be included for observation to the patient along with our standard use of drive and defence interpretation and demonstration of associative shifts from drive to defence.

I shall conclude this chapter with a clinical vignette.

"It's too fine for me!"

Ms B, who is in her mid-forties, is a long-time-divorced, high-level insurance company executive without children. She hails from a West Coast middle-class family in which her father was a college graduate and a mid-level civil servant and her mother was a housewife who had attended but not finished college and had, to the patient's puzzlement, done only menial work before marriage. Ms A's father died when Ms A was 18 years old and home from college for the summer. His death was due to an abdominal aneurysm that ruptured several hours after a fierce argument with Ms A's mother over money. Two years later, while again home for the summer as she awaited entry into business school, she fell mysteriously ill and was hospitalized for a month, with only a vague diagnosis of "some kind of collagen disease". Ms A is avoidant of her elderly and demented mother, who resides in a nursing facility in another state near Ms A's brother who is five years' younger than Ms A, is married, has children, and is a successful manager in a high-technology industry. Ms A described her relationship with her brother as one of indifference. She did not like his presence, and so as she grew up she pretended he was not there, a pattern she has continued. The patient completed undergraduate and MBA training in Ivy League schools without difficulty but also without distinction because she found it compelling to interrupt her studies from time to time to participate in various civic and cultural projects.

The patient's career advancement has been steady, but without satisfaction or pride for her. Irrational fears that she would be trapped in her marriage led to separation and divorce after four years. Affairs, some lasting many years, with married or otherwise unavailable men, relationships that she has felt a need to keep secret, have typified her love life. She is a social isolate who maintains contact with her female friends mostly by telephone.

Though she has a pretty face and a somewhat regal manner, otherwise good looks and gracefulness are compromised by moderate obesity. She often looks drained and tired, a fact she reluctantly associates with her alcoholism. She reported that she had had several prior treatments which had helped her. However, despite verbal fluency, she could not say how any of the prior treatments had helped her.

Ms A presented for treatment with a near panic level of anxiety and various somatic complaints, including backaches, skin eruptions, and repeated eye inflammations. Her opening words in the first session, accompanied by a smile, were the complaint: "I'm a mess." She agreed to work with me in a modified psychoanalytic way three times per week. Given her massive anxiety, her isolative nature, her regressive symptoms, and history of regressions on the verge of successes, I decided not to use the couch. She described her wish to get another professional position but said that she could not organize herself to do so.

Months of work focused on defence analysis of her lifelong tendency to back away from success was not very useful. For example, when she turned away from presentations to me of various ideas or images or evidences of success, the defences were demonstrated to her—often including pointing out how she turned aggression on herself—and efforts to identify the dangers necessitating such a defence were also made but to no avail. An interpretive approach such as pointing out her dread of her ambition, lest she surpass her mother and her father, also met with poor results. Of more value was the approach recommended in this chapter—that is, addressing transference of the total situation, by which I mean making as full use as I could of how it was the patient seemed to be using me with her words and nonverbally. For example, I brought to the patient's attention that she not only told me she was a mess, but that each time she did so, she smiled. I added that over time I had come to experience the two expressions as a search for me as someone who somehow would be pleased by her being in a disorganized state. In my own mind, I thought that my intervention was correct because of its apparent link to Miss A's mother. That is, I thought that in comparison to her mother, Ms A was afraid to realize her potential, out of guilt both about ignoring her demented mother and over surpassing her mother, who had never been particularly successful. Ms A's response confirmed that the effectiveness of the intervention had to do with its tapping into Ms A's internal representations of the mother as one who exacted from her a pledge not to be successful in life, other than to serve the needs of the mother. So, the patient had reached a compromise of this arrangement in which she had physically abandoned her mother, but not emotionally. The intervention led to the unfolding of two important memories, one involving the patient as a 3-year-old who loved to go to church because she could sidle up to a woman friend of her mother's after church and rub up against the woman's fur coat, which soothed her. She sadly realized she did not associate soothing with her mother. She hoped that by presenting herself as a mess to me, I would soothe and help to organize her. She also remembered that during her summer break from college at age 19, she went to the kitchen to tell her mother she was on her way out for a date. They argued over the mother's objection to a possibly flirtatious remark the patient had made to a long-standing male friend of the family in whom the mother was interested, now a year after the death of the patient's father. The mother then slapped the patient "so hard it drew blood". As the connection of these various experiences of the mother were worked through, she realized that her mother had transmitted to her the fundamental message that she as a woman, like the mother as a woman, should not advance and that any advance would be retaliated against, including any advance in relation to a man. Late in the working through process, she recalled something that the mother said many times over when she stopped herself from obtaining some pleasure or goal she wanted, and which the patient realized that she, too, had used as a mantra to limit her own advances. The expression was, "It's too fine for me."

Conclusions

The case of Ms A is intended to illustrate that interpretation of nonverbal memory—specifically, interpretation of her total transference presentation of herself as a mess, the statement and the smile—was the key to unlocking this patient's psychopathology for more effective work to be done. That work made it possible for traumatic events to be recalled (e.g. being slapped by her mother at age 19) and for the complex of feelings core to her difficulties to be expressed in words and be worked through. For example, she began to openly express to me her wish that I soothe her, versus previously having to sneak comfort, as she did at age 3, or demean herself as a condition for getting it, as in declaring herself a mess to me. As this work progressed, she realized more and more that the realizations of her ambition would not be too fine for her. That realization ushered in more reflection on her view of herself as a "mess". Slowly, she began to recognize the aggression in it—that is, by messing herself with self-rejection and with poor choices of mates. She also came to mourn the losses she felt in her messy early years, which she came to realize were bereft of warmth and support, especially support for her to be active, curious, and ambitious. With a considerable interpretive focus on Ms A's memories and fantasies associated with the church lady whose fur coat she furtively sought out, she eventually consolidated a more joyful conviction that she could seek out what she wanted openly and directly from people, with some hope of satisfaction.

As regards the more traditional ways of working, such as superego analysis, there is a role, as long as it is recognized that a patient's superego-determined expressions such as "I'm a mess" may have preoedipal origins and meanings that must be reached in the treatment. When they are, by interpreting the total transference situation, those patients who turn out to have, or who can gain stability at, higher levels of ego functioning may then be able to work in a more standard ego-psychological way, for example. That is, learning about the self-limiting ways they use their superegos to restrain their associations directed to the analyst may come to be usefully pointed out to them.

The glass ceiling's potential to deny women full development of their ambitions is great, but it is not all-powerful. Psychoanalytic treatment, properly focused, can substantially reduce its effects, because it seeks to rekindle the light underneath the search for fundamental human freedoms. Here I am reminded of Victor Frankl, an Auschwitz survivor, who wrote: "Everything can be taken from man [of course I include women] but one thing: the last of human freedoms—to choose one's own attitude in any set of circumstances, to choose one's own way" (quoted in Dionne, 1999). So, even in the likely irreducible circumstance of the glass ceiling faced by women in achieving fulfilment of their ambitions, psychoanalysis can enable them to choose their own way.

CHAPTER TWO

Glass ceilings, sticky floors, and concrete walls: internal and external barriers to women's work and achievement

Nancy J. Chodorow

Psychoanalytic consideration of how the glass ceiling is internal as well as external treads a fine line, since the concept was created precisely to draw attention to external causes. Originally, the glass ceiling was meant to describe structural and behavioural barriers to women's promotion. It was designed to correct a popular belief and common corporate defence, that women's lack of upward mobility was caused by fear of success, by non-competitive values and goals, or by other internally generated restraints and beliefs (Christine Williams, personal communication 2000). Of course, the glass ceiling is indeed internal as well as external. To the extent that sociologists and economists have repeatedly and in detail documented its externality, it seems that we as psychoanalysts can really only contribute to an understanding of the ways that glass ceilings are still—though in more complex ways than "fear of success"—also internal. And in so doing, we need to be careful, since there is always a danger that a focus on internality shifts the blame and relieves those with power and authority from the burden of instituting change.

The term "glass ceiling" began to appear in the mid-1980s; by 1991, the federal government had established a "Glass Ceiling

Commission" and instituted the "Glass Ceiling Act". This Act was designed to punish corporations that discriminate against women in the upper tiers. The metaphor is appealing, carrying with it the sense that what is immediately above—either an upper floor or, even, the sky—is reachable but that, when a woman tries to reach it, a glass barrier turns out to be in the way. In the 1990s, scholars suggested that we also needed to consider "glass walls"—that is, barriers to horizontal mobility across jobs and professions. Other commentators argue that metaphors like "sticky floors" and "concrete walls" better describe the rigidity and tenacity of glass ceilings. In this chapter, I consider a variety of external and internal barriers to achievement in women, beginning with the most blatant forms of discrimination and exclusion from without and moving to an indication, found in the consulting-room, of the great variety of gender-inflected personal expressions of self-limitation.

In order to deepen our inquiry, it is perhaps worth extending the concept of glass ceiling to refer to unnoticed or indirect assumptions and practices in addition to intentional discrimination. Psychoanalysis, I think, can contribute to our understanding of how and why these unnoticed, indirect assumptions and practices operate. On the most blatant level, we can look to concrete walls and ceilings, where men traditionally have simply kept women out, in power organizations like the male-only clubs or in the proverbial locker-rooms and on the golf courses where they conduct business. In explaining the male-bonding dynamics of these spheres and their need to exclude and belittle women, we cannot improve upon that still amazingly powerful psychoanalytic classic, Karen Horney's "The Dread of Women" (1932), or the more recent psychoanalytic feminist classic, Dorothy Dinnerstein's *The Mermaid and the Minotaur* (1976).

On a slightly less overt discrimination dimension, I turn to a *New York Times* article written by Natalie Angier (2000), who spoke with women astronomers about the "glass ceiling in the sky". Adding to the cache of metaphors, the article describes women "leaking out of the pipeline": of PhDs in astronomy, a larger percentage of men than women receive postdocs; of postdocs, a larger percentage of men than women become assistant professors. Apparently, the same thing happens in medical schools (Angier, 2000). The woman astronomer who has been looking into the glass ceiling in the sky has collected testimonies from her colleagues about being ignored in collegial conversations, being asked to do housewife errands for visiting scientists, and being stereotyped as cute little women who couldn't be interested in scientific puzzles. She notes that these are small slights and benign neglect, but that at the same time they are "molehills that gradually accrete into mountains". Angier also describes the conservative response, a response that returns from the external glass ceiling to two "internal" perspectives—the "free choice" and "wilting lily" accounts. First, according to her male scientific informant, women don't succeed in scientific fields because they don't like them and they don't excel in them. This is the "free choice" argument. Second, women are "less prone to the intense, cut-throat aggressiveness that usually marks the successful research scientist or engineer"—that is, they are "wilting lilies". Neither of these, you can see, involves straight-out discrimination.

When we turn to our own profession of psychoanalysis, we may be even further from outright discrimination and further in the direction of implicit stereotyping and taken-for-granted assumptions. We can note that only two women have run for (and lost) the presidency of the International Psychoanalytical Association (IPA). The IPA has elected only three women as Secretary. The American Psychoanalytic Association (APsaA) has elected only three women Presidents and appointed only two women as Chair of the Board of Professional Standards (and neither of these latter served in the last 35 years).

We certainly cannot assume in these elections that either losses or wins were a direct result of a particular candidate's being a woman, and we have also to note the softening of the glass ceiling in psychoanalysis that allowed these few women to run for office in the first place. Nonetheless, my own research on the role and impact of early (second- and third-generation) women psychoanalysts elicited an interestingly textured glass ceiling, porous in some places and firm in others (see Chodorow, 1986a, 1986b, 1987, 1989, 1991, 1999b). In both Europe and the United States (there is, of course, national variation here that I cannot go into, including the important British Society-saving presidency of Sylvia Payne), women were historically overrepresented as training analysts and underrepresented in official leadership positions—presidents of societies, chairs of training boards, and so forth. So, there was one arena—that of training analyst (some would say the arena of highest prestige and influence in the field)—in which stereotypes about women and women's own self-identities as excellent clinicians, as people who communicate well orally, as teachers and trainers, and as nurturers of the next generation, enabled women to reach the top, and another—that of elected or appointed position of power or authority—with a glass ceiling or sticky floor.

Noting the paucity of women in psychoanalytic politics, some of my women interviewees pointed out both that women were uninterested in the arcane and internecine psychoanalytic infighting and that men didn't want women leaders. Various terms emerged that spoke to the barely below-the-surface fear of strong women. One American interviewee described the "little patriarchy" at the Anna Freud Centre. An eminent second-generation British Middle-Group man who had great respect for the many women who had been leaders in the history of the British Society nonetheless described the Kleinians as a "phalanx of women, and they all wore black". A woman Kleinian concurred, claiming that Klein and her women colleagues were treated as "an awful regiment of women", and she described her relief when some men joined the Kleinian ranks. A man trained in the 1950s at the Boston Psychoanalytic Institute alternately described Helene Deutsch, Grete Bibring, Beata Rank, Eleanor Pavenstedt, Helen Tartakoff, and others as the terrifying "Boston matriarchy" and at another point in his interview as a "group of bubbies". Another very well-meaning third-generation interviewee, a former President of the APsaA and Chair of the Board of Professional Standards, claimed about all the women powerhouses with whom he had worked that they were "lovely women". He insisted, in response to some challenge on my part, that the woman Chair of the Board of Professional Standards with whom he had worked most closely "didn't have an ounce of politics in her body". We cannot know in specific cases if women are "too lovely" to be President of the International or the American, or Chair of the Board of Professional Standards, or if potential women candidates see themselves as part of an "awful regiment of women", or even if such considerations have had any substantive impact. But we can see in a general way how such attitudes, many of which are not in the first instance directed towards exclusion or channelling, could have contributed to a porous and uneven glass ceiling in the history of psychoanalysis, a glass ceiling fostered internally by women themselves and externally created collaboratively by both women and men.

I found myself, in writing this chapter, mulling over a personal example, which I bring forth because it comes with an emotional resonance that I think is part of the complexity of the glass ceiling as both internal and external. This example shows how unnoticed assumptions, or individually varying assumptions, can subtly perpetuate external glass ceilings, or, in this case, glass walls—here, professional rather than gendered glass walls. As I perused the brochure for the "Women and Power" conference, sponsored by several international, national, and local psychoanalytic associations, I noticed that I was listed exclusively as Professor of Sociology. I then reflected upon my assignment to a panel on the glass ceiling—a concept from sociology—when almost all of my professional writing has been in the psychodynamic areas of female psychology and development, maternality, femininity, and men's views of women. The conference organizers were clearly thinking that I had, in addition to my track record as a thinker about psychoanalysis and women, some expertise on the interface of psyche and society and that being a Professor at the University of California at Berkeley was a position of pride and eminence. My own (we could call it) professional countertransference reaction was to feel that I could not, finally, be accepted as a psychoanalyst. We can see here how even the most well-meaning "external" others—and each of us is an external other to some other person's "internal" identity and desires—can, because of preconscious assumptions, contribute to the perpetuation of glass ceilings.

So far, I have suggested that the externality of the glass ceiling moves from blatant, overt exclusion and discrimination to subtly stereotyping assumptions by well-meaning others. When we move to internal glass ceilings and walls, sticky floors, or even concrete ceilings and walls, it is much too simple, I think, to speak of one form of "internal" glass ceiling, as if all women have internalized the same assumptions about legitimate aspirations and ambitions. Rather, we are in the well-investigated realm of conflict, fantasy, and inhibition—internal glass ceilings engaged in by men as well as by women—as well as in the psychoanalytic realm that says that any choice or behaviour is a complexly created compromise formation that attempts to manage anxiety or other threatening affects. Internal glass ceilings are produced by many factors—by oedipal guilt, by anxiety about separation, loss, or castration, by those wrecked by success, by the spoiling and self-spoiling powers of envy, by grandiose, narcissistic fantasies that lead to fears of humiliation, by conflict about aggression, by self-punitive superegos, by survivor guilt, and by many other unconscious and conscious fantasies, all of these put together differently by different individuals.

Few psychoanalytic papers address the glass-ceiling phenomenon. A classic theoretical and clinical treatment of internal glass ceilings can be found in Joan Riviere's 1929 paper, "Womanliness as a Masquerade". In this paper, Riviere discusses professionally successful women who present themselves in overly feminine ways in their appearance and in their roles as wives and mothers and also women who work to appear incompetent, both patterns of conflict and behaviour being engaged in in order to deny and avoid punishment for the fantasy of achieving success through stealing the father's penis. These successful women want to masquerade, as Riviere says, "as guiltless and innocent". In "Some Observations on Work Inhibitions in Women" (1976), Adrienne Applegarth also describes several motivations for an internal glass ceiling, as does Ruth Moulton, in "Professional Success: A Conflict for Women" (1986). Most recently, Adrienne Harris's "Aggression, Envy, and Ambition: Circulating Tensions in Women's Psychic Life" (1997) describes how internally charged these three affects and desires are in many women, in relation to issues of separation or of feeling as though one's aggression and envy can displace and kill, and how all of these make achievement with pleasure and without self-punishment difficult.

Thus, any woman's internal glass ceiling is a product of her own subjective gender and sexuality—her conscious and unconscious fantasies about being female—as well as whatever else goes into her internal affectively charged world and her characteristic fears, conflicts, and defences. As I thought about my own patients, I could not think of one—male or female—in whom gender or sexuality did not contribute to an internal glass ceiling. I thought about women who felt that to do maths well was to be masculine or to invite male aggression, of men who could not play sports to the best of their ability or could play only defence but not offence well, for fear of oedipal victory, of women who thought that assertion was the same thing as destruction and killing, and so forth. So I thought I would look for a glass ceiling, a sticky floor, and a glass wall.

A glass ceiling

First, I remembered a woman, L, a law student, whose *internal glass ceiling* was a product of guilt, guilt at being able to have pleasures and achievements that her mother could not have. L had emigrated as a child with her parents. Her parents had an arranged marriage, but in their country of origin her mother had had a profession. After emigration, L's father did what was necessary to continue his profession, but her mother became a traditional subservient housewife, coping with her husband's patriarchal demandingness and difficulties in reestablishing himself and with her children's integration into a new culture. The father worked hard and was critical of his wife, and she became depressed, letting the house and cooking go and not paying attention to her own well-being and appearance. L did the work necessary to stay in school, but she kept herself from trying to get the best summer jobs and from shining as a student. And she could not take pleasure in her work.

As I have described for similar women from patriarchal societies, L "wept for her mother" (Chodorow, 1999a). She described how she could not make herself food, keep her apartment clean, or pay her bills, because she felt guilty for living on her own and having a future career. She felt that she shouldn't do these things if her mother couldn't. She reported that almost every time she found herself enjoying something—going to a late movie, wearing a sun dress, driving alone, looking down at the lights of the Bay Area—her next thought was "My mother couldn't do this," and she felt guilty and sad. She could not take pleasure or be happy in her achievements if her mother was not happy.

A sticky floor

I had a harder time coming up with a pure clinical example of a *sticky floor*, but I did think of another patient, C, who experienced a tangled stickiness in which so many factors intertwined in her attempts to manage gender, sexuality, and success that unproblematic work and advancement were difficult. This woman wanted to be successful, but she thought of success as totally masculine. Reflecting back on her childhood, she said: "Images of what it meant to be an admirable person were all male. Or there was the single, lonely, pioneering path to something women don't do, the few successful women, like Jo, in *Little Women*. She's the most interesting character in the book—she's a tomboy; she strides everywhere. There are no men in the book; her father is away. Then, she's transformed through love into a real woman who's married and has children." When I asked about that, C replied, "Defeat! The end of the line! Maturing for women is being transformed in a way that puts a damper on her activity, turns her into a wife and mother. That's all there is: accept your fate, your limitations. 'Accepting fate' is part of maturity. Being tamed into a wife and mother, giving up fantasies of being powerful, important, and active. The other side is getting a man, of your *very* own! Giving up *being* a man, or the hope of being a man, for *getting* a man. Where are heroic images of women *as women*? I'm stuck in a desire for heroism, for recognition, acclaim, being admired."

As we looked at her dilemma—that if she finally became an acclaimed and admired hero she would become a man—C said, "I guess it's the only way to get there," and she cried, saying "but then, there's the fear of retaliation: if you're assertive or aggressive—that's me, competitive—it's also associated with men. In the books, you're a prince; you don't *have* to compete if you're a prince—your position is already assured. In our society, there's competition, and it's frightening."

C once described a meeting that ended up being only women, and she noted how impressed she was with their competence. She said, "it wasn't a kill-or-be-killed model of interaction, but I'm not committed to it. I'm stuck in the kill-or-be-killed model. I didn't know how to behave in that setting. I'm more comfortable in the other—what I gloss as men, but it's not only men. I know how to handle myself in situations with lots of direct challenges to ideas. It doesn't make me happy, but it's involving. I feel prevented from fitting into a more flattened landscape, one without hierarchy. If its not up or down, on the way up, or on the way down, struggling against being put down, I'll disappear."

So C didn't have an emotional or intellectual space for competent yet non-hierarchical women, and she felt that her own aspirations and ways of thinking and preferring to interact were masculine. But these aspirations themselves created conflicts. She liked and didn't like the kill-or-be-killed model, and she was always worried that she would be brought down as a woman if she used it. "If you're feminine and passive," she claimed, "you're too weak, not tough enough to be in the world. Dependent." She wanted to be "top man on the totem pole" and "one of the boys" at work, and she wanted acknowledgement and recognition of her position from male co-workers. But the problem was that wanting recognition was itself dependent, putting her right back in the feminine and weak place she was trying to escape from. So it was a loss either way, a reminder that she was female if she couldn't be top man on the totem pole, or that she depended on men to acknowledge her top manness, which reminded her of her femininity.

On another occasion, C got herself into a tangle by emailing a complaint about a sexist remark made by one of her colleagues to her whole unit, because she thought her response was so clever and sophisticated. Then, she felt extremely vulnerable and open to humiliation, finding that wanting to have flashy and sexy prose too easily collapsed into feeling that she was displaying herself sexually and fearing humiliation. Her oscillation between fantasies of intellectual power and flashiness and potentially humiliating sexuality continually left her upset and brought her professional life to a standstill.

A glass wall

As a last example, I want to describe a therapy session involving an *internal glass wall*—a patient's, S's, inhibitions against moving from one field to another. S has a full-time job in a field in which she was originally trained, but for a time she left another secure job in this field to go to graduate school in painting—her first love—in order to become a painter. But now, she doesn't do any painting. S was describing how she would let down her boss, who is also a friend, if she quit her job or went part-time, but that another friend from graduate school in art had just phoned to say how much she and her friends loved S's work, how they wanted to see more of it. It was clear that the conflict was not just between wanting to paint or having to work at a secure job.

I asked S if she could just think about painting—what images, memories, or fantasies came to mind. Her first association was in Spanish, though she is not a native speaker—the word *ociosa*, which, after some reflection, she was able to find in English: that painting—indeed, all the visual and musical arts—was for the "idle rich". She went from there to a Marxist boyfriend she had had in Mexico who said that only the rich could study the arts, then to a protest song about an "ociosa" housewife with servants and a landlord husband, who was contrasted with a Jesus-like man saving the poor. S has also told me that she has a good voice and used to love to sing in public, but that she doesn't do so any more. Just as her friends represented either side of the painting/job dilemma, S's husband, from a culture in which women don't display themselves, is seen to be the one who keeps her from singing. S said that in graduate school several students had once noticed that only she and one other student hadn't gone to private art schools as undergraduates: they hadn't been rich enough to do so. But then she associated to starving artists in garrets in Paris, to *La Bohème*, and to Gauguin giving up being a banker in order to become an artist in Tahiti.

Another conflictual image surfaced: she wanted to live a bohemian lifestyle as an artist, but she remembered seeing a famous woman artist in an elevator in Manhattan on the way to this woman's art-show opening, and the artist was in designer clothes. Art openings led to further conflict: she imagined going as an artist to parties and salons with other artists and poets and then, in an arena that is very charged for her, having to be brilliant and witty. I reflected back to S all the different meanings of painting in itself, and she replied, as she became very teary, that she had an image right then of being, every day, in her studio, how that would be such an amazing, wonderful life. She remembered the same bursting into tears when she told a co-worker years ago that she was leaving her job to go back to painting. I said that it seemed to me that it was unbearable, in some way, for her to think about painting daily, in her studio, and she said, still crying, that it was the ultimate risk. So, here we can see someone who has two career identities, and it is a very complicated glass wall—a glass wall that can be seen even in one session's work—that keeps her from the career that she consciously most wishes to pursue.

* * *

Clinical vignettes never make an argument, but my point has been to note that once you get down to individuals, it is not clear exactly what it means to be talking about "the" glass ceiling being internal. Achievement, success, wearing a sun dress, painting, being a good lawyer, rising to the top, being unproblematically competent and non-hierarchical can all be conflictual goals, and they are tied to images of femininity and sexuality, to images of mothers and fathers, to fears about risk, to selfhood and identity, to culture of origin. These internally created glass ceilings, glass walls, and sticky floors meet those generated by layers of externally created barriers, constraints, exclusions, and expectations, and they meet explicit and implicit assumptions about women in general and about particular women in particular times and places.

Acknowledgement. I am indebted to Christine Williams (personal communication 2000) for all the information on the history of the concept of the glass ceiling and for the alternate metaphors of limitation and self-limitation that I consider in this chapter. A psychoanalytic sociologist, Williams has written several books on gender and work, looking especially at men and women in cross-gender jobs (1989, 1995). She coined the term "glass escalator" to describe how quickly men rise to the top in female-dominated professions (1992).

CHAPTER THREE

The internal glass ceiling

Miriam Tasini

During the past thirty years many changes have taken place in the status of women in our society. Four times as many women currently enter professional schools as did in 1970. Yet women are still underrepresented at the higher echelons of academia and industry. Two recent studies—one of women on the faculty at MIT (Hopkins, 1999b), the other of women on the faculties of U.S. medical schools (Nonnemaker, 2000)—revealed that women continue to occupy primarily the lower faculty ranks, as demonstrated by the data in Tables 3.1 and 3.2.

The discrepancy is even more striking when looking at percentages. At MIT, women comprised 29% of graduate students, 22% of junior faculty, but only 6% of faculty at the professorial level (Table 3.1). Women occupy only 11% of board seats in major corporations (Hopkins, 1999a).

Social factors are not to be ignored as causative of these discrepancies. However, in view of the changing social fabric, a question has to be raised: how much of this apparent disparity might be the outcome of internal psychological conflicts that inhibit women from competing in the same way as do men? The problems of work inhibition in women was first addressed by Adrienne

Table 3.1. MIT School of Science: Distribution of Women at Each Stage of Career

	Biology		*Chemistry*		*Cognitive science*		*Mathematics*		*Physics*	
	F	*M*	*F*	*M*	*F*	*M*	*F*	*M*	*F*	*M*
Graduate students	101	118	73	176	17	36	17	95	30	267
Post-doctoral	27	57	20	71	18	34	2	5	3	12
Faculty	7	42	2	30	4	19	1	47	4	77

Source: Modified data provided by Lydia Snover, MIT Planning Office.

Applegarth (1976) twenty-five years ago. At that time, she presented an overview of the internal factors that prevent women from moving out of their homes into the working world and seeking careers. Like Applegarth, my work is based on data obtained from long-term psychoanalytic and psychotherapeutic treatment. The current discussion addresses work inhibition in women in the context of significantly different external realities. The focus is limited to unconscious identifications and inhibition of aggression that lead to the formation of what I call the "internal glass ceiling" . How do these identifications and inhibitions affect women's competitive professional efforts? How might they be modified in the course of psychoanalytic treatment?

"Identification" is derived from the Latin word *idem,* meaning "the same". Freud (1950 [1892–1899], Letter 58) began using the word in 1897 to mean, most broadly, being or becoming mentally like someone else who serves as a model in one or more respects. Identification is not simple imitation but, rather, a structured modification of the personality or character of the person who does the identifying. In psychoanalysis, we usually refer to "identification with". The earliest identifications are with loved and admired parental figures. Identification with others who are admired, loved, feared, or envied continues to occur through childhood, adolescence, and, we believe, adulthood. We postulate this as part of the unconscious modification occurring during analysis: old identifications may be altered and "abandoned" (Compton, 1985).

Some identifications may be incorporated into the superego. Other identifications, less likely to be involved in conflict, become part of the "stable character" or ego. When the conscious or unconscious wish to be or act like another becomes a source of fear or other unpleasure, however, the ego will mobilize defences and an alteration of behaviour, a compromise formation, will result. With whom, and how, do women—more specifically, professional women—identify? Are there patterns of identification that are more likely or less likely to promote or facilitate competition and success? What differences can we discern in the nature and outcome of processes of identification among women who compete and succeed as compared to women who remain assistant professors without making a conscious decision about their status?

Table 3.2. Distribution of Women at U.S. Medical Schools

PERCENTAGE OF WOMEN MEDICAL SCHOOL GRADUATES, 1971–1997

1971	11%
1979	23%
1997	41%

WOMEN PHYSICIANS IN ACADEMIC MEDICINE, 1979–1997

	Men	*Women*
Total number of graduates	235,776	71,495
Total entering academia	21,940	6,030

Academic Advancement

			Women	
	Total	*Men*	*Expected*	*Actual*
Associate professor	4,959	3,940	1,374	1,019
Professors	590	460	105	59

Source: Modified from Nonnemaker (2000).

It appears that the degree of conflict in the area of a woman's professional pursuits correlates, in several ways, with her relationship to and identification with a successful mother and/or father. I shall attempt to clarify how these identifications may intertwine with expression of aggression in the competitive work arena. Expressions of aggressive drive may become morally prohibited in many women. Parens, in his direct observational studies of children (Parens, 1990), reports that there is no observable difference between girls and boys between ages 2 to 4 years in the expression of hostility. He states, "Four year old girls are every bit as aggressive as boys; they are as hostile and as assertive, demanding and tenacious as boys." He found that from that time on, however, a quantitative difference between boys and girls begins to appear in the discharge patterns of aggression. He separates aggression into components of non-destructive aggression, which fuels assertive and goal-achieving behaviour, and hostile, destructive aggression, which generates rage and hostility. According to Parens, women appear to lack a clear separation between goal-achieving competitiveness and destructive, forbidden, primitive rage. Continuing his study, Parens leaves us with a question of the origins and causes of inhibition of assertiveness and the presence of relatively heightened passivity in many adult women. I hypothesize that identification with a competitive, achieving, yet nurturing and benign parental figure provides clearer separation and allows a relatively conflict-free career pursuit. However, if the parent is seen as not benign but destructive, the identification may lead to increased guilt over aggression and subsequent repression of competitive striving.

Identification is not the whole story regarding conflicts about competition. Focusing solely on identifications will leave out crucial issues such as core-gender identity, penis envy, and the formation of the girl's Oedipus complex. The women who are described in this chapter demonstrate a spectrum of conflicts in the arenas of professional achievements and interpersonal relationships. The origins of these conflicts will be explored followed by speculation about how these conflicts may be altered in analysis with a woman analyst, as well as how the transference relates to the failure or success of such modification.

"Gladys"

Gladys, aged 28, came to treatment after moving to Los Angeles to start a new career. Her call to a former therapist, requesting referral to a "married woman", was prompted by a break-up with a man with whom she had had a brief affair. She had not been able to sustain a relationship during the preceding nine years. She also had periods of depression precipitated by objectively minor mishaps. An intelligent, educated, and sophisticated woman, surprisingly she never attempted to obtain any additional personal or professional information about me. Later in analysis she described a fantasy about me that eliminated any of my professional status or credentials. She saw me as a loving and loved wife with an ideal family. This made me indistinguishable from her grandmother, mother, or younger sister, all of whom were educated at prestigious institutions but never worked for pay. She saw these women as attractive and desired by men, as opposed to herself, a working professional woman.

When first married, the patient's mother was given a large endowment while her brothers entered the family business. The patient's father managed the money that belonged to the women in the family. He pursued an advanced degree and, by the time the patient was born, had started to rise in his chosen profession, becoming a respected and prominent member. He is described as controlling, angry, volatile, critical, and self-absorbed. The patient's mother appeared as a shadowy, frightened, unassuming woman. She deferred to her husband and tried to arrange family life to accommodate his needs. Until recently her life seemed to be a cultural stereotype: perfect hostess, mother, wife, and community volunteer.

The patient is the second of four sisters. The oldest sister holds two advanced degrees and has been very successful in her work, which is related to the father's profession. She is single. The third sister was seen as a helpless and fragile baby by the family. She married upon graduation from college, never worked, and has three children. The family myth was that she had an untroubled, perfect life. The youngest sister was still attending college at the time of the analysis.

As I pointed out earlier, conflict configuration is influenced by identifications with important figures other than parents. The patient had a close friend with whom she shared her life almost daily. The friend's father, whom the patient referred to as uncle as he was a distant relative, was famous and was admired by the public as well as by the patient. He was a significant influence in both her childhood and professional career. This man admired her talents and encouraged her creativity. When she began her professional endeavours in an area distantly related to his work, he continued to be helpful and supportive. In addition, this man's wife was a very successful professional.

One of the patient's conflicts was between wishing to be a passive, loved female attached to a husband versus being a successful, working professional. This was reflected in fluctuations in the transference, seeing me both as a competent, professional, independent, masculinized physician and as a married woman, dependent on a husband, valued as a kindly mother but insignificant outside the family. The latter was related to her request for a married woman analyst and continued as a theme for several years. The patient seemed to want to reinforce that side of her identifications. Initially, I did not pursue this assiduously. Rather, I avoided the subject because of my own distaste for this stereotype of a desirable woman. As I worked to bring her rigid and extreme view into focus, she began to observe her need to avoid and distort reality about me in order to preserve her view of what constitutes a desirable woman.

When she became anxious after a major promotion, her fantasies about professional success in the corporate world were explored. She believed that becoming prominent in her industry would not only turn her into a man, but also make her undesirable and threatening to men. The following interaction demonstrates the conflicts and process of change:

Analyst: "You are saying that you do not believe any man could find a professional woman like you—or like me—attractive. I guess you believe your father or any other man would not give me the time of the day either."

Patient: "Oh, no, he would like you, but only if he did not know you were a doctor."

She realized that she did believe that her father disapproved of, and therefore could not love, a successful woman professional. She was ambivalent about losing her father's love if she proceeded with her professional goals. Her view of herself, me and all working or unmarried women slowly changed as she was able to recognize it as stemming from her wish to be loved by her father and wanting to be like him. A modification occurred as the analysis progressed and she became more aware of the distortions she had created about her analyst. She recognized that her analyst wore a ring on her left hand which she had not previously noted. This realization made it easier to identify with the ideal object/analyst in the transference who could be loved and yet be a different kind of woman from her mother.

Identification with the values of both parents with regard to proper roles in life for women, and identification with her mother as role model, were in part responsible for her inhibiting her talents and her inability to translate her aggression into career competition and success. Identification with the values of her father as a model for competitiveness formed the other side of the conflict, expressed in terms of models and identifications. She played all of this out in fantasies about her analyst and the analyst's imagined husband. In the transference, she was unable to make demands upon me, fearing I would be too fragile to respond. Her major defence was reaction formation, leading to a fiercely independent stance. She despised her mother's passivity and inadequacy and was terrified by her father's unmitigated aggression. Her ability to seek other parental figures helped her in some measure to compensate for the parental deficits.

Throughout the years of analysis, the trials and tribulations of her work carried on. She continued to hide the fact that she clearly excelled in her work. Being competitive and aggressive was inconsistent with her mental representation of an ideal woman persisted. This recurrent struggle to present herself as a passive and giving caretaker prevented her from openly reaping the rewards of her work. For example, she hid her successes from me and from the woman who was her boss but whose performance was inferior to that of her own. Her fears of retribution and loss of love were analysed when her boss lost her job and the patient was offered the position. She wanted this woman to love her and treat her as a friend. Consciously she believed she would be ostracized and hated. The analytic interventions allowed her to recognize the guilt associated with her unconscious wishes to eliminate the competition.

Her father's inability to express affection freely or regularly left her bereft of the ability to feel lovable to a man. His hostility towards women made him a dangerous object. During the analysis the recovery of loving feelings for her father, as well as his admiration of her and her sister's accomplishments, led to acceptance of her masculine identification with him. Her recognition of her mother's suppressed anger led to modification of her image of mother as the ideal passive, self-sacrificing saint, allowing the patient to seek pleasure with less guilt. Her recognition of her envy of men minimized her need for self-deprecation. In addition, through her identification with me, or her fantasy about me, she resolved the need to rigidly segregate traditional male and female roles and functions. This freed her to express her aggression in a goal-directed fashion and no longer fear that her accomplishments and successes would make her undesirable. In the fourth year of analysis, she married. Her previous unconscious belief that she could never be loved unless she was the "perfect woman" like her mother was finally overcome. Competition that allowed the sublimation of her aggression, formerly seen as threatening to her mother whose love she feared losing, became more acceptable.

"Helen"

Helen was a graduate student who was in the process of a divorce when she first sought treatment. Her mother was a prominent professional with national reputation. During the patient's childhood, her mother often travelled around the world to give presentations and earned considerably more money than the patient's father. Her father, who had a PhD, was a professor at the community college in the town where she was raised. Her parents divorced when she was 11 years old, and her mother remarried.

To her mother's dismay, the patient married shortly after graduation from college. She was an average student although very talented in a special form of performing arts. This was not viewed either by her or by her parents as prestigious or as "a real profession". She entered graduate school and worked while pursuing an advanced degree in an area that was associated with her mother's profession.

Initially she saw her mother as the symbol of perfection and was critical and contemptuous of her father's passivity and lack of prominence. Unconsciously she feared her mother, seeing her as devouring and dangerous. Consciously she wanted to be like her mother, tough, hard working, invincible. She was contemptuous of her father, viewing his artistic pursuits as weakness. As the analysis progressed, she was able to recognize her love and attachment to her father, who had provided most of the nurturing during her childhood. Her identification in her professional pursuit was with her father, who was an artist, as well as with her mother, the academician. Her unconscious fear in competing with her mother was of being destroyed, a fear described in men who are unable to compete with their fathers as castration anxiety.

Towards the end of the third year of analysis, she was talking about her fear of destroying someone by being angry, when an earthquake struck. She stood in the doorway, a safe place away from the windows, trembled, and started to cry. She looked at the analyst standing next to her, who was clearly also terrified as the building continued to shake with after-shocks. She was astonished that the analyst was frightened. This became a recurrent subject in the course of analysis. At times she laughingly wondered whether her omnipotent wishes brought on the tremors to scare the analyst. She was concerned about whether she could trust the analyst to help her, knowing she was "not an analyst just human". The discovery of this imperfection was disturbing: the fantasy that she preserved of an ideal object, a perfect, invincible mother, was shattered. Previously she had recognized intellectually that the identification with her mother led her in a perpetual search for perfection. She was never comfortable in any situation in which she felt she was unable to imitate parental behaviour. Seeing the analyst as vulnerable and human, different from her (image of her) mother, allowed her a new identification that helped her feel acceptable and separate. She described it as having a sensation of "hatching", experiencing a "sense of freedom not to have to always follow rules". She gave up the pursuit of the advanced degree in the area of her mother's work but pursued another advanced degree. She remarried. Following the birth of her child, she returned to creative activity.

"Lucille"

Lucille was a 34-year-old corporate lawyer, a partner in her firm, who came to see me because her six-year marriage was deteriorating. She had been raised in a small town where her father was the chief of police. Her mother came from a minority group and was an uneducated housewife. According to the patient, her mother was very beautiful and always preoccupied with her appearance. Lucille did not recall feeling close to her mother as a child and had a contemptuous attitude towards her as an adult. Lucille was an exceptional student from a very early age. Her father admired her abilities. He prized her accomplishments and encouraged her to go to law school, his own unfulfilled dream. She was his confidant from a very early age and recalled spending long hours hearing about his work and asking him to review her school work. Her mother was uninterested and uncomfortable in the father's political circles. From age 12 years on, the patient accompanied her father around the county on law-enforcement business. When she was 14, he suffered a nearly fatal heart attack, followed by several other cardiac episodes that forced him into early retirement. It was unclear whether her mother was unable to manage the family affairs and finances, but these were turned over to Lucille by the time she went to college. She often returned home on weekends to help her father with family finances. He died shortly after her college graduation.

Following her father's death, the patient managed her mother's affairs. She became her father. She never expressed any ambivalence about professional struggle. She had been offered an academic position but chose the corporate world. That allowed her, as she put it, to claw her way to the top, which she did without evident ambivalence or fear. She ascended very rapidly in her chosen area of law.

The man she married was a businessman, only marginally successful. He allowed her to manage their financial affairs, and she became the main income-producer. Their conflicts increased. He left her for another woman. She showed very little distress, sold the house they owned, and "moved on". She proceeded to date, but the men she chose or attracted were never her professional or intellectual equals. This led to numerous painful experiences that became the central theme of her treatment. She left treatment briefly when her negative feelings towards her father began to surface. She realized that she wished he had cared more genuinely for her rather than loved her as a prized possession who would fulfil all his dreams. She realized that neither parent ever treated her as a "baby". Her mother's narcissistic concerns were about her own and Lucille's external appearance. Lucille, like her mother, was very attractive. She appeared to minimize her beauty, thus avoiding any similarity to her mother. She saw her mother as incapable of caring for another human being. She returned to treatment after becoming involved in an automobile accident that could have threatened her life and her career. The need for medical attention allowed her to be cared for, briefly, without undue anxiety. She realized in the subsequent months that she felt she could not be in any way like her mother and expect anyone to take care of her, especially her analyst. Lucille did not appear to have any ambivalence about the importance of her career. She became the first partner among her group of "litter mates". She competed mercilessly with both men and women for prestige and recognition. It was not only her identification with her father, but also his loving and condoning attitude towards her achievements that appeared to have eliminated any guilt or conflict about her career path. Her difficulties stemmed from her need to repress her dependency needs. She equated this with becoming like her mother, whom she viewed as a helpless, denigrated, sex object. She was unable to form lasting relationships, including the one with the analyst, in which she feared becoming passive and dependent. She left treatment.

"Martha"

Martha was a 40-year-old business executive who was moved by her corporation to head a new subsidiary office. She became severely depressed six months after this move. When she sought help she was preoccupied with constant worry about neglecting her children or letting down her company. Martha's father was a prominent European politician. Her mother gave up a law career to raise her family and manage the many moves her husband's work required. She was assiduous in the care of her two children. Martha viewed her parents marriage as a "happy partnership". Neither she nor her brother showed evidence of academic or interpersonal problems. She had several long relationships while she ascended the corporate ladder. When she described her work success, she said: "I was a born politician like my father." She felt close to her mother, whom she seemed to admire.

She had been married for six years and had two children, aged 2 and 4½ years. Her husband was an academician who was willing and able to participate in the child care. She had the financial resources to secure child and household help. She refused to have a housekeeper live with the family, because she thought she should be the one to put her children to bed every night. She insisted on attending "Mommy and Me" classes, fitting these into a schedule complicated by national and international business negotiations.

The therapy became another demand; she often missed sessions because of either job demands or "the needs" her children. The therapeutic effort was directed towards exploring her need for self-sacrifice in order to meet her criteria of perfection. In one of her early sessions she struggled with the feeling of obligation to attend a birthday party of a relative on the West Coast on Sunday and a corporation meeting on the East Coast on Monday. The initial solution was to take a very late flight on Sunday night.

Martha experiences a common struggle among professional women whose early identifications with parents are relatively conflict free in the work arena, but who are unable to integrate mothering, caretaking roles with their roles in a competitive work environment. There appears to be an inability to modify inflexible demands for perfection in all areas of endeavour. Martha's attempt to be a perfect diplomat, like her father, and become a perfect parent, like her mother, failed. She felt inadequate, angry at herself for her failure, and depressed.

Discussion

I have limited this presentation to the area of identifications and how the different identification constellations may lead to work success or work inhibition. The dominant parental identification may be with either parent. I have described four different conflict configurations.

Competition in all areas of human endeavour, including work, is a derivative of aggression. The aggressive components can be superego-sanctioned or prohibited. Women appear to have greater superego prohibitions against direct expression of derivatives of aggression. Overt aggression is equated with masculinity. It is not sanctioned by the cultural (group superego) standards. Aggressive women are referred to as "bitches", less than human, unlovable.

Studies that might clarify the origin of such gender differences are inconclusive. Galenson and Roiphe (1976) concluded from their infant observations of differences in muscular activity that boys are innately more aggressive. Parens (1990), however, indicates that parents encourage the expression of assertiveness in boys and passivity and compliance in girls. This would certainly lead to different conflicts and compromise formations in men and women in competitive work situations. Such compromises would be influenced heavily by identifications with parents who are successful and seen as allowing and even encouraging competition. Perceptions of parents as destructively aggressive and competitive may inhibit the formation of positive identifications.

My discussion, like the one by Applegarth (1976), is based on the limited but rich data of analytic experience. In order to obtain more corroborating data, study of a larger population of working women would be necessary. Such a study would have to include a survey of women who do not seek treatment as well as a larger sample of working women who do seek psychotherapy.

I am left with many unanswered questions about the work success of future generations of women.

THE NAVEL
Maternal power

CHAPTER FOUR

Mothers and power

Joan Raphael-Leff

Each and every one of us throughout the generations anywhere in the world has slithered out of or been retrieved from a powerful woman's body. We too swam in an amniotic sea within a swelling uterus, punctuated by the booming sound of a life-giving heartthrob until, vernix-coated, we were propelled headfirst along a tight birth canal, or lifted out from within a slashed belly. Thus, nary a one of us is exempt from the originary mother's power.

Therefore, in most societies since human time began, whether received with joy or caution, birth has been regarded as an awesome primal event. It is the moment when one becomes two or more, as the still-tethered hidden being emerges and, severed into separateness, begins its solitary course towards mortality. Left alone, the infant would surely die, for all human infants are born prematurely, unable to fend for themselves. We who have survived infancy have thus all been dependent on the power and generosity of nurturing (m)others.

These are the axiomatic facts. All else varies—how birth is conducted, how the cord stump is treated and the placenta disposed of, how the newborn is received and by whom, where she or he is placed and when fed, attitudes to colostrum, feeding, sleeping, crying, care are not "accidental" but are determined by cultural, temporal, and personal variations. Similarly, powerful forces external to the infant define who those crucial "others" are, whether a group of women or a singular one, the biological mother, her female substitute, or a nurturing man or sibling. And cultural mores influence the nature, distribution, and subjective meanings of their caregiving activities—from feeding, holding, bathing, soothing, smiling, teasing, scolding, cajoling, and so forth.

The archaic mother

In non-traditional societies, rather than a community of caring mother figures it is often one *specific* woman to whom we each surrendered and against whose authority we gradually revolted, humiliated by what Dinnerstein (1976, p. 166) called the "profoundest prototype of absolute power" over our bodily weaknesses. The fantasy of omnipotence granted the primary powerful caregivers is condensed into the one named maternal figure—"Mummy". Contemporary psychoanalysis finds that if this archaic mother's power is absolute, it is not only because she holds the physical balance of life and death in her hands. Indeed, she lays down future physical health and immunological protection through her placenta, breast-milk, and the diet she provides but, perhaps more importantly, in the mental nutrition she offers and the power struggle she represents.

The primary caregiver forms and informs the very constitution of a child's psychic reality. Not merely by meeting needs for intimacy and comfort as classical theoreticians suggested, but, I suggest, by *intersubjectively moulding and defining the very criteria that organize self-evaluation of these needs.*

The power of the maternal body

To Freud, the ego is "first and foremost a bodily ego" (Freud, 1923b)—a mental projection of the bodily surface, which, traditionally is primed and serviced by the caregiving mother. Ministering to the infant's body, she activates the mental apparatus while laying pathways for future sensual interchanges. I would add that this usually occurs at a time when not only is she dealing with the neonate's primal substances, but her own body is highly charged and sensitized by child-bearing. Fertile, lactating, bleeding, and aromatic, the maternal body is empowered with primitive female mysteries. Some French post-Lacanians (such as Kristeva, Irigaray, Cixous) argue that the archaic relation to the maternal body acts as metaphor for undoing paternal repression. A "semiotic" mode of polymorphous rhythmic bodily forces and unrepresentable psychosomatic expression originate in prelinguistic communion with the mother, which underpins and at times acts to subvert symbolic signification. I would argue that in Western societies, which valorize autonomy, *dread of archaic maternal power* (of the many kinds I elaborate here) and anxiety about *yearned-for emotional re-engulfment in the originary symbiotic unit* persist as a constant intrapsychic and cultural impetus towards illusory separateness and misogyny, the breakdown of which often occurs in child-bearing.

In this chapter I trace some consequences of the fact that in industrialized societies, due to urbanization, geographical mobility, breakdown of extended families, and changing social mores, women often mother alone in isolation, having lost their own network of support. I argue that, paradoxically, this psychosocial change both *increases the individual mother's power over her children* but simultaneously *exacerbates her own vulnerability*. The powerful mother is herself at risk of being overpowered by emotional forces inherent in the child-bearing/rearing situation.

Power of the biological mother

Given effective female-based contraception and access to legal and safe abortion, we may also say that each Western child today is indebted to the mercy of the biological mother—not only that maternal caregiver who accommodates her self-interests to those of the child, but the woman who has tolerated that flesh to grow within hers, and decided to sustain life rather than abort it from within her fertile womb. Today, these may no longer be one and the same. A woman may be the child's *genetic mother*, or an *ovarian mother* who provided the egg but not the womb, a surrogate *uterine mother* who incubated someone else's egg to term, a *birth mother* who gave life but not mothering, an *adoptive mother* who herself suckles and/or cares for the baby, or one who appoints someone else to do so on her behalf. The mother may be single or in a stable relationship with a male or female partner or be part of a child-raising commune. Despite contraception, many pregnancies are unplanned, and, with those that are, motivation for conception varies—wanting proof of fecundity, desiring a pregnancy, the wish for a child, or compulsion to actualize an impossible dream.

Modern mother's power

Today's woman has the power to make extraordinary decisions. In the last half century, in addition to complex sociopolitical developments, there have been dramatic changes to seemingly eternal facts of life. Earlier menstruation, assisted conception, donated gametes, and postmenopausal reproductions; multiple births due to ovarian hyperstimulation; same-sex egg exchange and gay parents; twins born years apart; pre-implantation diagnosis and corrective foetal surgery or abortive "reduction"—all mean greater complexity of this decision-making process. Elsewhere, I have suggested that these new reproductive techniques may also be used to realize unconscious fantasies in relation to "generative identity"—to magically reverse anatomical limitations of gender, generation, genesis, or generativity and/or to actualize oedipal desires or play out ideas of parthenogenesis or rebirth (Raphael-Leff, 1997b).

In Freud's view, the symbolic order is predicated on "victory of intellectuality over sensuality" (Freud, 1939a [1937–39], p. 114), as a father accepts a child as his own without cord-linked evidence of genetic connectedness. With surrogacy and egg donation, motherhood too is now exposed as the "fragile social construction" (Derrida, 1994) it always was rather than a biologically predetermined "maternal instinct". Thus, in the absence of hidebound traditions, we are more aware that in addition to unconscious psychosomatic mechanisms of reproduction, a human mother is a *subject* in her own right, who uses her own thinking power to make procreative and other decisions. Never simple, as the Darwinian Hrdy (1999) remarks, there are always intricate "tradeoffs . . . in a world of constantly shifting constraints and options" (p. 376).

Conscious decisions about *whether, when, how, and with whom to have a baby* involve juggling timing and costs of socio-economic subsistence, gauging the bodily toll of pregnancy and lactation, and the emotional requirements of her various loved ones as well as her own future professional and reproductive prospects. Rational as these decisions may seem, they are also underpinned by unconscious psychic fantasies and residues of her own infantile experience as well as current psychosocial pressures.

The powerful perinatal mother

Even *in utero*, interaction is complexly systemic, shifting from mutuality to alienation. A "power struggle" may ensue to achieve balance between mother and foetus, particularly in relation to that aspect of the embryo that is a genetically foreign body to her own. In turn, the foetus is responsive to the force of maternal factors through hormonal fluctuations; diurnal variations in movement; and vestibular, dietary, thermic, and gustatory influences, including emotion and intonation, (Chamberlain, 1987) revealing a discriminating sensory system and memory for specific prenatal stimulation. In the days following birth, innate behavioural systems in the vulnerable newborn are activated and reinforced by smell, touch, taste, and the voice of the specific primary caregiver, which he rapidly comes to re-cognize (De Casper et al., 1987).* For his own survival, the baby must become exquisitely sensitive to signals of this ambivalent caregiver's power—counteracting signs of indifference, preoccupation, or hostility by initiating activities to engage and charm her into caring (see Trevarthen, 1980).

*I am using the linguistic convention of a masculine pronoun only to differentiate the functions of carer and infant—which could, of course, be reversed or same-gendered.

The ambivalent caregiver

In a paper way ahead of its time, unlike many idealizing psychoanalysts Winnicott (1947) acknowledged maternal ambivalence, citing seventeen reasons why a mother hates her baby. He added that the important thing is her capacity to *not act* on it but to hold on to and survive her own hatred, as she will survive the baby's attacks on her without retaliating. Elsewhere he made a crucial distinction, stressing that while the baby could use maternal ambivalence as a spur to growth, he could not deal with her repressed unconscious hostility (Winnicott, 1969). However, her own survival of his assertion of omnipotence enables recognition of her separateness and non-retaliatory existence. I argue that in this intermediate area between reality and fantasy, conversely, in her restraint and survival the mother, who has been stirred up by both the infant's attacks and her own infantile destructiveness, gains a measure of her own internal resourcefulness.

However, I propose that in addition to her feelings of exploitation, persecution, and rejection by her seemingly unresponsive or critical baby, and as well as rivalrous competition with her own mother and deprived envy of her baby's mothering, a contemporary mother has a further source of frustration. Her ambivalence is also fuelled by *discordance between her egalitarian ambitions and the needs of her baby, which have changed little over the millennia.*

In the West, where the mother has been schooled from an early age to believe in female emancipation and self-actualization, there are further reasons why she may resent a male partner's capacity to reproduce without physical side-effects and without the conflict work obligations and competition over resources that their joint offspring's physical and emotional demands present. In addition, these may reactivate profoundly intense feelings of deprivation and envy of her child's mothering, or rage, rivalry, or remorse in relation to her own mother's competing or contrasting mothering style.

If to Freud (1940a [1938]) a mother's power lies in being both "nourisher and first seducer", we must acknowledge that many a modern mother also "feeds" her child unconscious conflicts and frustration over her own professional and personal desires. Social idealization of motherhood pathologizes ambivalence, promoting self-castigation, guilt, blame, and shame in mothers who become aware of their inevitably mixed feelings. I argue that when *unformulated resentment accumulates, it is unwittingly transmitted as a background sense of adult non-fulfilment, critically sensitizing a child's unconscious self-image* as obstruction and thwarter of maternal desires (in the way that the mother's enigmatic eroticism—Laplanche, 1995; R. Stein, 1998—sensually arouses her child's awareness of secret sexual knowledge beyond his understanding).

If maternal power may be broken down to its originary, archaic, biological, perinatal, and caregiving constituents, its true source lies in an infant's hyper-dependent malleability and in the gradual process of unconscious introjection through which his very identity and sense of self is constituted. Elsewhere, Winnicott (1971) suggested that the mother's face is the baby's mirror, that what he sees reflected in her face is how she feels when she looks at him. But what happens if the mother reflects back not the child she sees but a fantasy baby of her own making, her own rigid defences, or, what Winnicott does not mention, an aspect of her own baby-self that is still seeking gratification or revenge? In other words, the mother's powerful "mirror", like those at fairgrounds, is only as true as its distortions allow. When she substitutes her own "gesture" for the infant's, investing him with aspects of her own psychic life, that baby might compliantly opt for *her* version of himself (what Winnicott, 1960, called "false self"). Disavowing evidence from his own perceptual and proprioceptive experiences, he lives with the dissonance of vicariously *becoming* the idealized or derogated baby in the mind of the caregiver. Conversely, if she enjoys mothering and is empathetically attuned to her baby's needs (Emde, 1989; Stern, 1985), through their interactive exchange the mother's sensitivity will sensitize him to emotional understanding of both his psychosocial states and her own, and to awareness of the implications of people having feelings, thoughts, and minds.

Increasingly, we have come to recognize how much the developing organization of a child's experience is a function of the child–caregiver "*system*" (Sander, 1977), in which by reciprocal influence (Beebe & Lachman, 1989) and "graduated" failure a trusting mother relegates to the child increasing control over self- and mutual-regulation. Indeed, when the primary carer is able to sustain a maternal "reverie" (Bion, 1967), through a complex process of contemplation of her feelings and internalization of her reflective capacities the infant will come to develop his own capacity to reflect, think, and understand the moods, thoughts, and emotions of others.

This is so provided that both she and he share a common external reality that not only gives him an exciting "triangulating" acquaintance with the real world but enables him to recognize how their responses differ in relation to any specific object in it (Cavell, 1993). Thus, through cognitive understanding and emotional reception of unconsciously disseminated experience, the baby imbibes the mother's tacit assumptions about how the world works, who is friend or foe, and what to accept or avoid, thereby creating what Bowlby (1980) called the child's "internal working model" of expectations. Simultaneously, while alerting him to his internal states, the mother unwittingly transmits psychic substances of her own inner world, and within it, residues of her emotional ancestry for incorporation by the child (Raphael-Leff, 1997a).

Power of the past

Formation of subjecthood is further complicated for the child when the caregiver *herself* cannot differentiate between her projections, ascriptions, and the subjective feelings of the infant and acts upon them. Sadly, we are also coming to recognize all too well the power of mothers to abuse their position of power when, caught up with their own past abusive experience, they turn the child in their care into an object of absolute domination or sexual gratification. A mother who is psychotic, depressed, borderline, and hypersensitive to demands or persecuted and emotionally preoccupied with her own childhood is unable to participate fully in the mutual exchange, leading to distortions in primary interaction that have been shown (Murray & Cooper, 1996) to persist long beyond the mother's illness. Her own excessive need for control, her domination or defensive inhibition, her unresponsive "deadness" (Green, 1986) and lack of capacity to contain and reflect, her own misattribution, denial, or impairment of emotional understanding (Stern, 1985) all in turn affect the child's development of reflective-self function (Fonagy, 1995) and empathetic understanding, resulting in serious psychological limitations. This brings me to my penultimate point.

The powerful mother as disempowered subject

A mother's intersubjective relationship with her baby is doubly constituted: emotionally coloured by mental representations of maternity rooted in her own affective experience of being mothered (which I shall address later), and socially, economically, and politically primed throughout her life by maternal exclusions from, as much as authorizations of, power. This contradictory idealization of motherhood yet denigration of mothering forms a substrate of maternity. The emotional climate of the household of a woman's infancy unconsciously transmitted by her own parents in every dominant or submissive gesture and tone of voice not only predetermines her future sense of entitlement to be a mother in her own right with the blessing or forbidding presence of a usurped archaic mother, but the agential or marginal status of that very maternal position in relation to society.

In her stance, energy, facial expression, tone, mode of breastfeeding, caressing touch, and crooning words a mother conveys critical information to her own infant not only about his lovability, but about her sense of self in relation to him, as a disempowered woman empowered only by her relative power over him, as a passive or dominating instrument of socialization or as a person of recognized standing in the world.

Thus, the sociopolitical arena is reflected in the bubble of babycare, in an intergenerationally transmitted, subjective, lived experience of what motherhood and the baby signify to her, and to her mother before her.

The emotionally overpowered mother

The final issue I deal with here is that of the emotionally overpowered mother. I argue that maternal power is counterpoised by the power of the infant over the mother. As I suggested earlier, postindustrial social stratification leaves a new mother unsupported and ill-prepared for mothering while fostering an intense dyadic relationship to her baby—a dyad in which she is both immensely powerful but also vulnerable to reactivation of her own infantile experience at the very time of greatest demand on her adult capacities within this highly emotive situation. The baby's raw feelings and her own direct dealing with primal substances (amniotic fluid, lochia, colostrum, urine, faeces, milk, mucus, vomit, etc.), create a regressive pull towards primary interaction of that which she has absorbed from her own mother's child-bearing body and unconscious representations. A new mother suffering from what I have termed "primary maternal persecution" (Raphael-Leff, 1986, 2000) may in fact be so immersed in unresolved early scenes with her own archaic mother and siblings that she is unable to engage robustly with the baby in her care.

A mother's unprocessed generative experience, her unconscious female "carnal knowledge", and untransformed inner constellation thereby form a powerfully biased instrument in shaping the new baby's psychosexual body and self-image out of the stuff of her own infancy and primary caregiver's unconscious representations. In other words, *maternal power is embedded in a chain of transgenerational representations*—of the new infant as one's imagined baby-self in the body–mind of the original carer coupled with the unconsciously internalized archaic mother's view of herself as both caregiver and corporeal woman in society, and as infant mirrored in *her* own mother's mind. These unconscious representations interact with immediate contingencies such as sex, birth order and spacing, number and origin of offspring, quality of paternal commitment, available extramural assistance, environmental conditions, local mores, and other changeable factors influencing one or other side in the ambivalent balance of a mother's crucial choices—of whether her baby will live or die, whether to keep this child or have it fostered elsewhere, whether to mother exclusively or delegate care and by whom, whether to allow herself to fall in love with her infant or to create defensive conditions to emotionally detach herself or even to spurn it.

In conclusion, I have argued that the power of mothers over their infants is not merely bodily but resides within the child's unconscious internalization of transgenerational forces of unprocessed maternal psychosomatic representations, powerfully revived in the unsupported mother herself within the child-rearing situation. More than ever before, we have become aware that in their pre-conceptual, pre- and postnatal life-and-death decisions, women do not simply blindly obey their hormonal dictates, drives, or psychosocial interdictions. Each mother's stance is a delicately balanced compromise formation between often-irreconcilable pressures of multiple internal figures and external dependants, personal desires and unconscious forces, and constant awareness of the clash between the seductive pull of the baby's unmet needs and urgency of her own. If our own mutative power as psychoanalysts is to be helpful, it lies in recognizing the complex contradictions of maternity for today's mother and baby and by offering both of them a safe place to explore these rather than promoting unachievable theoretical ideals.

CHAPTER FIVE

"What kind of a mother are you?" Reflections on the film *A World Apart*

Ellen Handler Spitz

> "We were kept very separate. They said they were trying to protect us, but really it was easier, simpler, not to have to explain things to children . . ."
>
> Shawn Slovo, filmmaker
> (from an interview in London: Buntman, 1995)

In March of 1986, I ran to the telephone feeling sure it would be my sister calling from Virginia to discuss last minute preparations for the dinner we had planned for our father's 85th birthday. The family was about to gather to honour its eldest living member at an event that had taken months of long-distance negotiation. Each of the grandchildren had prepared a surprise treat, including original poems, speeches, songs, and compositions for violin, oboe, and harp. The voice I heard on the other end of the line, however, was not my sister's. It was the gentle voice of my daughter Jennifer, calling me from New Haven, where she was a student at Yale. "Mother," she asked softly and unforgettably, "will you be very upset if I am arrested tomorrow?"

During the preceding months, large numbers of Yale undergraduates had been protesting their university's practice of investing its funds in companies that were continuing to do business in South Africa despite that nation's abhorrent racial practices. A number of Jenny's friends were planning to take part in massive demonstrations in front of Beineke Library, and the police were expected to be out in full force. Student detainments had already occurred. Trying to sound composed, I told her I wanted her to do what her conscience dictated but begged her in the same breath to try not to be in jail the day of her grandfather's birthday celebration.

Jenny did participate in the demonstration but, as it turned out, there were few arrests that day, and she was able to arrive in time to address the guests at dinner. When it was her turn to speak, she rose and fervently described the suffering caused by apartheid in South Africa. She told us about the student protest movement in which she and her friends were involved and about the shanties they had put up on campus to demonstrate living conditions in Soweto and in other areas of South Africa restricted to people of colour. Finally, she turned to her grandfather and told him that, as far back as she could remember, he had encouraged her to stand up for justice and to seek it.

Two years later, the film *A World Apart* was first released,* and Jenny telephoned me this time to ask if I would go to see it with her. We went, and it moved us both deeply. It seemed to me to be about South Africa but also about much more. I saw it as dramatizing the painful conflicts that many women (and our daughters) face when we attempt to do important work in a world that often misconstrues, constricts, and disempowers us, while we, at the same time, continue to perform our ongoing duties within the homes and families in which our feminine powers have traditionally been vested.

---

*The film *A World Apart* (Atlantic Entertainment Group and British Screen, 1988) was written by Shawn Slovo, produced by Sarah Radclyffe, and directed by Chris Menges.

This, then, is the background of my initial exposure to *A World Apart*, a film as timely today as when it was originally released, a film that takes place in the South Africa of 1963, in Johannesburg, between the Sharpeville Massacre of 1960, when the African National Congress was banned, and the Rivonia trials of 1964, when Nelson Mandela and others were sentenced to life imprisonment on Robben Island. The screen play is by Shawn Slovo, eldest daughter of the eminent South African Jewish activist-journalist Ruth First, whose life is fictionalized in the film (as the character "Diana Roth"), and the prominent Communist activist Joe Slovo ("Gus Roth"). Shawn herself is called "Molly" in the film, and her two younger sisters, Gillian and Robyn, are also portrayed in it. Basing her screenplay largely on her own vivid memories, Shawn Slovo drew also on her mother's memoir, *117 Days* (First, 1965).

As background for the film, it is helpful to know that Shawn's parents belonged to a group of immigrant and second-generation Jewish intellectuals and activists in Johannesburg who were vehemently opposed to apartheid and who joined the Communist Party in the 1940s and 1950s in part because they saw Communism as the only political ideology that was colour-blind. The circle of activists with whom the Slovos associated included many prominent figures, including Rusty (Lionel) Bernstein—who became the model for Nadine Gordimer's character "Burger" in her celebrated novel, *Burger's Daughter* (1979)—as well as, of course, Walter Sisulu and Nelson Mandela.

Although the action of the film ends with a reunion and reconciliation between mother and daughter, the audience is informed in a final statement that Ruth First was, in fact, subsequently murdered. After prolonged detention in prison, following banning, house arrest, and stifling suppression (everything she wrote was forbidden), she finally departed from South Africa with her children for London; it was only later on, when she had returned to Africa alone to continue working against apartheid, that she was heinously murdered by the South African Special Branch police, who, in 1982, planted a time bomb in her mail, causing a fatal explosion.

For me, the principal subject of *A World Apart* is the tearing *apart* of a mother and daughter in the context of societal fragmentation—of racial, social, national, ideological, cultural, and linguistic apartness. I see this film as focusing on the distortions that occur, the unavoidable pain that is endured, when the normally uneasy psychological processes of early adolescent separation—daughter from mother—take place in a sociopolitical matrix that induces, exacerbates, and derails them all at once.

Fourteen years have passed since the film appeared and won its accolades at the Cannes Film Festival. In the interim, many political changes have occurred both in South Africa and in the world at large, and yet there is far too much, worldwide, that has *not* changed and that therefore makes this film as pertinent today as when it first appeared.

Mother and daughter

A World Apart focuses on a particularly delicate moment in the rapport between a mother and daughter—namely, the period of pre- and early adolescence, when a girl is on the verge of becoming a woman and when, consequently, there may erupt between the two a tense renegotiation of their power relations. (For an exploration of these cataclysmic changes in the mother–daughter relations, I know of no finer novel than Jamaica Kincaid's *Annie John*, 1986.) In this film, power seems to manifest itself—to the young girl Molly—by her mother's withholding information from her. Her mother is keeping secrets. Parenthetically, we may recall, in this context, Freud's young adolescent patient Dora who, similarly, resented the fact that information and knowledge were being withheld from her (Freud, 1905e [1901]), and we may also remember the strained relations between daughter and mother and their secrets so poignantly described in the unexpurgated wartime diaries of 13-year-old Anne Frank (Netherlands Institute for War Documentation, 1989). The theme is an important one. In retaliation for these "secrets", whatever they are or are thought to be, but also in order to protect newly forming boundaries from encroachment, girls of this age often close themselves in and hide, begin to contrive secrets of their own (e.g. the locked diary, the bolted door, the whispering voice) and to withhold information from their mothers.

In *A World Apart*, Molly refuses at one point to tell her mother the contents of a conversation she has just held with the headmistress at school. Explicitly, she conceals this information as a retaliation, but in this case what is interesting is how the normal developmental situation is complicated and exacerbated by the political conditions under which it is occurring. Diana—as a committed and imperilled journalist bravely reporting on the atrocities taking place in her country—*cannot* reveal the precise nature of her work to her daughter nor can she disclose the details of her comings and goings. To do so would be to place them both at even greater risk. She must keep secrets out of necessity. Molly's father, for the sake of security, has disappeared. After watching him kiss Molly goodbye at the start of the film, we never see him again. And his absence cannot be discussed by mother and daughter. Not only can Diana not tell her daughters where their father is nor reassure them about his return, but she herself is in darkness and in doubt. Thus, the developmental imperatives, already sensitive, are fraught with additional baggage; the ante is upped, and the audience too is left in ignorance.

We see, further, how the necessity for silence, brought on by these political considerations, can exacerbate a child's sense of isolation. We know that early adolescence is often a lonely time for girls. Their bodily changes and new-found distance from their mothers frequently give them a sense of estrangement. They become aliens in a self and a world that has metamorphosed into unrecognizability. Molly feels doubly abandoned by Diana, who seems, inexplicably to her, to care more for complete strangers than for her. This too fits with the developmental trajectory, since, as girls pass through the stages of puberty, they often sense they are losing privileged status with their mothers, a status previously conferred by being, as very little girls, compliant and non-threatening. Some preadolescents in fact retreat to this position and try to stem the tide by retaining elements of girlishness; others plunge headlong into rebellious adolescence where a different kind of privileged status beckons, one that may involve heterosexual exploration and not, initially, a close alliance with their mothers. This latter arena, however, is fraught with added difficulties for Molly. As the child of South African activists, she has no stable parental relationship to witness, no secure family structure in which and out of which to grow.

At a gala party thrown by her best-friend Yvonne's mother and father, the two girls, arrayed in their party clothes, participate in this adult social function, and Molly's behaviour is revelatory. Whereas Yvonne—after being boisterously caressed and admired by her effusive mother—boldly asks the boy next to her to dance, Molly does not follow suit. Feeling awkward and alone in this debonair world, having watched Yvonne go off to dance she then retreats from the party into the kitchen where black women are cooking and serving and accepts their offer of something to eat. In this way, she pulls back from adolescence and at the same time imitates her own mother's involvement with the non-white population. Her regression is immediately noticed by Yvonne's mother, who, in a kindly, overbearing manner, shoos her out of the kitchen and back to the party, where, however, she is then made to suffer a humiliating attack on the part of Yvonne's racist anti-Communist (and possibly anti-Semitic) father.

The direct expression of feelings must also go underground in the Roth family. Molly's anger at her mother cannot be easily expressed. After the ninety-day detention Act, under which Diana is precipitately hauled into prison, leaving Molly and her two little sisters parentless and under the care of the hired woman, Elsie, and their maternal grandmother, there is, simply, no more mother around to get angry at. By way of substitute, Molly aggresses against her visiting grandmother. She behaves so rudely and oppositionally that, at one point, the grandmother says to her: "Sometimes I think you have no heart." Molly is simply acting out: she is trying to make someone *else* feel as helpless, left out, and unloved as she does. She also behaves harshly to her siblings. Because no attention is being given her by the only people in the world who really matter, she cannot give it to anyone else. Not being mothered, she has no resources with which to mother her younger sisters. Nastily, she shoves them out of her room. In each of these scenes, her behaviour constitutes a replay and a reenactment of the situation she is in and cannot escape. Via substitutes, she perpetrates what she is forced to endure passively in the mother–daughter relationship.

Apropos of the suppression of feelings, this imperative to keep them under control is made explicit right at the beginning of the film. As Molly's father leaves her, possibly forever, for his unknown destination, his final directive to his aching young daughter is: "Be cheerful." The same message is reiterated by Diana later on when, referring to the police, she instructs the children not to cry in front of *them*. And the squelching of emotions is also required by Molly's grandmother when, on their visit to the prison, she says to her daughter Diana: "Are you crashing? We're counting on you." Interestingly, those words were actually spoken by Ruth First's own mother Tilly under the real-life circumstances on which the film is based. So, a conspiracy of silence, then, was imposed, as is usual under conditions of tyranny—a silence that works insidiously not only to force people to part from one another, but also to part from themselves, in the sense that by not acknowledging one's actual feelings, one begins gradually to lose touch with oneself and to forfeit a sense of personal integrity, to become increasingly vulnerable to destructive forces from within and from without.

Good mother/bad mother?

I would like here to compare two of the mothers depicted in the film, Molly's and Yvonne's, and to consider them in terms of the so-called *good-mother/bad-mother* split. Right at the beginning of the film. Yvonne's mother, a buxom blonde Afrikaner, arrives to pick up the girls at their private school in her large white sedan. As they traverse the crowded Johannesburg streets, they witness a horrific "accident", in which a black man is run over by a car and lies bleeding on the pavement. Molly is terribly upset and wants to do something immediately, but Yvonne's mother drives on saying, "I don't want to get involved." Thus, we have here a mother who is *good* in the sense of being available to fetch her own daughter and that daughter's chosen friend from school, but who is *bad* in that she remains cold and indifferent to what happens to anyone else, anyone outside her charmed circle.

When Molly is dropped off at her mother's office a few minutes later, we see a different kind of mother. Diana is too busy to greet her daughter with even a semblance of warmth. Deeply preoccupied with the problems of the black people, she has no time, interest, or attention left for Molly. She will not even let Molly tell her what has just happened in the street. We have, therefore, in these two women, a polarization—perhaps *the* polarization that has been mythologized in our culture. Women are either at home, fully, or they are not. I am reminded of Dickens's Mrs Jellyby of *Bleak House*, the notorious female do-gooder, who is willing to sacrifice anything for the poor people of Borrioboola-Gha but whose own children are pitifully neglected.

The sharp contrast between Diana Roth and Yvonne's (unnamed) mother is also represented in visual terms: Diana is dark, serious, slender, moody, and secretive, whereas the other mother is fair, mirthful, affectionate, and warmly expressive. Interestingly, and very authentically, both mothers manage to irritate and embarrass their preadolescent daughters—Diana by not being present at all, Yvonne's mother by being overly present and intrusive (she practically smothers Yvonne, for example, in the party scene). I think it also not without relevance that the fictional Roths are Jewish, as were, of course, their real-life counterparts. The blond hair of Yvonne's mother versus the black hair of Diana Roth might even evoke for some viewers the Marguerite and Shulamite of Paul Celan's 1947 poem "Todesfuge". The women are in some ways foils for one another and in other ways twinned. I see them as opposite in their spheres of function—Diana choosing to seek power to do good in society at large, whereas Yvonne's mother exerts her influence within the limited sphere of home and family—yet twinned not only in the complexities of their relations with their respective daughters but also in their helplessness in the face of masculine authority and dominance.

Diana, for one, is driven to the brink of suicide by her male tormentors in the South African jail. Similarly, Yvonne's mother fails to prevail against the cruelty, bigotry, and irrational rage of her husband. This is demonstrated in a scene where Molly walks to their home to try to rekindle her friendship with Yvonne after Molly's ostracization at school has caused a rift between them.

Yvonne's father bullies and chases her, despite the protestations of his wife. Thus, both women, although strong and forceful, prove no match for male dominance here—either in the home or in society at large.

In one early scene, at the Roth house, Molly and her younger sisters are playing outside when two strange black men arrive unexpectedly, one of them being, as it turns out, Elsie's activist brother Solomon, who has just been released from prison. The men ask to see Mrs Roth, and Molly obediently interrupts her play to lead them to her mother, who is working behind closed doors and who snaps angrily at her for interrupting. When, however, Diana looks past Molly and sees the two men who have arrived, her expression abruptly melts from a scowl into a charming smile; ushering them into her sanctuary, she closes the door pointedly behind them, oblivious to her daughter's hurt and puzzled face. So, we may ask: is it true that to be a good person outside the home one must be, at the same time, a bad mother? The model persists. It hurts especially here because, at this age, identifications are highly complex for young girls. Their earlier sense of congruity with their mothers has begun to give way. Rejected by her real mother, where does Molly turn?

Not surprisingly, she turns to Elsie, a kind and gentle woman who is, however, almost totally disempowered. Separated from her own children, who live in poverty in Soweto, residing in the Roth home for the sake of her job she can do almost nothing to protect or nurture her family except to work far away from them. Molly retreats to Elsie's room, sits on her bed, and learns her songs and a few words of her language, and, at one point, Elsie shows Molly some photographs of her absent children and repeats their names. Molly looks at them and at Elsie and asks gently: "Are you sad?" Thus, a bond grows between them, but it is, to some extent, a bond of the helpless. It is also Molly's way not only of finding a substitute *good* mother in place of her *bad* one, but also of connecting obliquely to her own mother by getting close to one of the people whom her mother is trying so earnestly to help.

When Molly goes with Elsie at one point to visit her family in Soweto, we see that she cannot successfully substitute an identification with the black community for what is missing in her own life. Just as, in the party scene at Yvonne's house, she was chased out of the kitchen and back to the white folks' gathering, likewise, in the scene in Soweto, Molly fails—despite the warmth of her hosts—to fit in. She sits politely at their simple table at dinnertime but cannot bring herself to eat the chicken foot she finds floating in her soup, even when it is explained to her that this is considered a delicacy. She observes the warm and respectful relations Elsie and her family have with their old blind grandfather, a stark contrast to her own discourteous relations with her visiting grandmother. Solomon, who is there with them that night, wants to make Molly feel welcome and accepted and praised. Intending to do so, he says to her and of her: "Molly is strong like her mother." Thus, she realizes that, even here, she cannot escape her destiny. Even from within the black community, she hears words that thrust her back to the place she needs to be but is finding it so difficult to be. Elsie functions, perhaps, like Yvonne's mother, as a *good* mother in contrast to Diana Roth, but she too is flawed, for she is profoundly powerless and, ultimately, is an unsatisfactory role model for the confused young girl.

Preadolescence

The significance of close friendships in preadolescence is well-known and is exemplified in the novel *Annie John* (Kincaid, 1986), where the young girl's succession of friendships track her gradual movement away from an early total absorption in and adulation of her mother. Cultivating an intimate "best friend" can assist a girl to segue gracefully out of her mother's orbit before developing mature social and sexual relations of her own. In Molly's situation in the film, however, the radical politics of her parents and the political climate of her country bar her from this crucial area of functioning. Her abandonment by Yvonne is one of the cruellest moments in the film—cruel, especially, because it is so poorly understood by Molly herself and because the defection has nothing to do with her per se but is a direct (and unanticipated) result of her parents' opinions, decisions, and acts. She is snubbed by her classmates and excluded from their company, and her closest friend, who at first defends her, fails in the end to remain loyal.

Meanwhile, her parents, who have unwittingly caused this, have, as we have seen, also deserted her. In addition, Molly has been betrayed in a sense by her own body, which is now rapidly changing. We see her, for example, at one point, studying herself in a mirror and powdering her face with her truant mother's make-up. We see her showing off her new grown-up hairdo to Elsie. In preadolescence, girls need extensive contact with each other and with encouraging adults so as to feel reassured about the physical as well as the psychological changes they are undergoing. For Molly, living in loneliness under apartheid in South Africa, the normal expectable quantum of disorientation becomes extreme.

There is also, of course, an intense curiosity and embarrassment about sexual relations in preadolescence, a theme that the film captures in several scenes. In the absence of both parents and in their absence from each other, Molly at one point fantasizes them dancing romantically together. By creating this lovely image for herself, she retrieves the model she so badly craves: the intactness of the parental couple. Early on in the film, before she is imprisoned, Diana hosts a bi-racial party for her activist friends (a party that, incidentally, is raided by the police). Yvonne and Molly are in attendance. Watching and whispering, the two girls sip from glasses of wine. Just before the raid, the camera, panning the guests, zooms in on a black and white couple kissing. Molly tries to hide this behaviour from Yvonne by holding up her wine glass so as to shield her friend's face. Here we see how typical preadolescent discomfiture in the face of adult erotic behaviour is exacerbated by the political climate, by the laws of apartheid that make such activity illegal. Molly's shame is doubled.

We know, furthermore, that school often creates problems for young people of Molly's age, in part because what was once a relatively benign, unquestioning respect for the older generation and its rules may give way to a more oppositional stance. With bodily shifts come further transformations. Once again, *A World Apart* demonstrates how political conditions complicate the normal state of affairs. Molly refuses in school, for example, to sing the national anthem. This occurs, however, immediately after she has witnessed her home invaded and searched by the Special Branch police. She is uncomfortable, too, with the headmistress of her school, who, while superficially kind and solicitous, seems to

Molly a representative of the very system that has rejected and victimized her family and therefore a potentially dangerous and untrustworthy individual.

When one of Molly's teachers patriotically intones the glorious history of South Africa, Molly stares absent-mindedly out a window. Her mood and action (with a mother in jail and a father gone) are clearly complex, but the teacher interrupts her monologue to ask pointedly: "Are you with us, Molly?" Breaking the ensuing silence, another girl vindictively answers: "No, she's against us." This moment seems highly fraught because it reduces what are in fact recalcitrant ethical and psychological puzzles to a stark dualism: *for* or *against*, *white* versus *black*, *good* over *evil*—the typical strategy of every tyranny, which is to close off thought by labelling groups, condemning some and idealizing others. Fortunately, after one has done that, one no longer needs to think. One is freed from doubt, liberated from the weight of one's anxiety. By permitting her student to denounce Molly with impunity, the classroom teacher acquiesces in this insidious tendency to polarize; she demonstrates her own participation in the regime of oppression.

Twinning

Another interesting aspect of *A World Apart* is the way in which it sets up a kind of twinning of Diana and Molly. Mother and daughter are, in a variety of ways, subtly paired, so that when something happens to Diana, something similar occurs in Molly's life; Diana's world, in other words, is actually mirrored in that of her eldest daughter.* Although the audience viewing the film can observe this phenomenon and the strong sense of dramatic irony it creates, this mirroring remains almost completely obscure to the characters themselves. Shortly after the police raid their home and verbally assault Diana, for example, Molly's former school friends insult her and call her a traitor. In a later set of scenes, just after Diana has

*In my essay "Mothers and Daughters" (Spitz, 1991), I discuss the twinning of mothers and daughters in texts ranging from the ancient Greek myth of Demeter and Persephone to contemporary American fiction.

been interrogated yet again in prison and is beginning to experience the desperateness of her situation and her aloneness, Molly is shown being abandoned by her best friend, Yvonne, who goes off with another girl, leaving Molly bereft. In yet a third set of paired scenes, egregious male violence against both mother and daughter are portrayed: one of the most brutal of Diana's interrogators slaps her face roughly in jail when she refuses to answer his questions; Molly is, similarly, verbally abused, threatened, and chased by Yvonne's racist father in his car as she runs in terror to escape him.

As I have indicated above, Molly is thus forced to suffer for her mother's moral choices without fully understanding them and therefore without having the opportunity of making up her own mind whether to concur with them or not. What the film makes strikingly clear is that, whereas adults are capable of accepting their elective deprivations because in fact they *are* elective—that is to say, chosen with open eyes—and because, as adults, we understand something about past and future and therefore count with conviction on the potential long-range benefits to society of our sacrifices, children, on the other hand, have no comparable vision of the future and therefore do not feel strengthened and ennobled by deprivation. They may be, contrariwise, like Molly, disempowered and depressed by their parents' behaviour and its consequences to them. Parenthetically, the young actress who plays Molly in the film conveys this depressive affect tellingly by inclining her head, walking with a listless gait, and drooping her shoulders (again, a stance that is overdetermined considering the age of the girl). What empowers the mother Diana, in other words—her sense of commitment, choice, and trust in the future goodness of her acts—works exactly the opposite way with respect to her daughter Molly.

As case in point, when Diana is arrested and is being led away from the house, Molly cries out in a broken voice: "Please don't go, Mommy!" This is significant, in that the language used at this moment implies that on some level the girl still imbues her mother with the power to go or not to go. Of course, Diana Roth is *compelled* to go. Yet, the way Molly continues to see her is as a powerful mother, as *her* mother. And she desperately needs Diana to be strong, not only because of her own developmental requirements but because she too has by now suffered and has effectively just this one parent left to support her. Consequently, it is very difficult for her to grasp the reality: namely, that her mother has been reduced to a victim and is now completely in the hands of the hated and feared police. She does not say, for example, "I won't let you go," or "I won't let them take you away." Her utterance expresses the abject helplessness of her own situation—her unmet needs, her losses. Her anxieties overwhelm any other possible mode of awareness or functioning at this moment.

A part or apart?

In the final section of this chapter, I would like to contemplate the notion of the word *apart* and its ambiguities. In the beginning of the film, Diana clearly feels she is a part of something significant—a great movement with freedom as its goal. She is energized by her mission. She is one with it. Furthermore, she sees herself as carrying on the work of her husband, Gus Roth, a passionate, effective revolutionary. She and he are living apart during the time recorded by the film, but they are also a part of the worldwide Communist movement. In prison, when Diana finally breaks down under pressure and attempts suicide, she writes in her suicide note that she cannot let Gus down. Yet she is also a part of a family—the mother of children. Who will be left to care for and raise those children if she is gone? Here we discern levels of complexity, for although on a manifest level she indicates that her relationship to her distant husband and commitment to their comrades trumps her motherly love, this can only be a part of the story. Does being *a part* of one thing imply being *apart* from something else?

In real life, Ruth First's own parents, Tilly and Julius First, were radical socialists from Latvia and Lithuania, respectively (Frankel, 1999, pp. 45 passim) and, as the character of the grandmother in the film reveals, they were deeply committed to the values they had passed on to their daughter. Thus, Diana's moral choice in attempting to take her own life was not inconsistent with what had been espoused in Ruth First's actual family; yet, even as such, the act seems problematic.* What does it mean that Diana shows herself ready to die in order that others may not die on her account (lest she break down under torture and reveal their names), ready to honour her pledge to her husband and to place these moral imperatives on a higher plane than her obligation to her three young children? What kind of a mother *is* she? Interestingly, her act is not portrayed in the film as one of uncomplicated heroism and martyrdom. It is portrayed as a complex gesture compounded of enervation, desperation, cowardice, and shame and even of guts and of shrewd calculation. For although Diana is reviled by the police for having broken down, she is immediately attended to by them on that account; they proceed without hesitation to save her life and to release her from prison.

Why do they do this? Why is Diana sent home after her suicide attempt? Largely, I believe, because she is a woman. Never, under such circumstances, would they have released a man. Her jailers, as I read the film, want her to submit, to give in. They want, above all, to humble and humiliate her, not to destroy her. They ask her, for example, at one point, whether she misses her children (*sic*). They taunt her: "All this playing Joan of Arc is only an excuse for being a terrible mother," and, later, "You've wasted your life; you could have done so much." So, I think it was her courage and defiance that incensed her male interrogators. Once she had broken down, they were able to be finished with her. And we see here a confluence of feminist and racial issues, for, as a woman, Diana had privileges accorded her that were given to no black male prisoners; they, without quarter, were brutally tortured and murdered. This contrast is made explicit in the film through the tragic figure of Solomon, whose suffering we must witness directly.

Ultimately, under apartheid, no one was exempt from suffering: even those who thought they were gaining lost.

* * *

A World Apart captures the way this cruel system deformed one mother–daughter dyad in a family that was struggling to change its society for the better while maintaining itself as an intact unit of

* These issues are debated along gender lines in Aeschylus' *Oresteia*.

that society, and how this project became impossible. The final breakdown of the mother in prison can be regarded as symbolic of the family's failure as a whole to remain undivided under the impact of external centrifugal forces. The film, however, presents us with an extreme case of a situation with which none of us is entirely unfamiliar. Its moral choices are *not* apart from our own. What kind of mothers, fathers, and children are we, and how do we balance the weights of our own manifold responsibilities and the far-reaching consequences of the choices we make? These are questions that, explored sensitively in the film, extend in relevance far beyond the boundaries of South Africa and beyond the *mise-en-scène* of Shawn Slovo's still disquieting film.

* * *

As I gaze back on the events that inspired this chapter, I appreciate even more fully that it was my own daughter Jennifer's engagement with the student protest movement and her embrace of me that drew me in and provided the spark. Without our cherished relationship, the chapter could never have been written. Education flows back and forth between a daughter and her mother—when they are both blessed with ongoing life. Like Shawn Slovo, I too lost my mother in an untimely fashion, and these days I watch anxiously as my daughter tries to cope with her own variety of the struggles depicted in *A World Apart*.

THE WOMB
Creative power

CHAPTER SIX

Women, creativity, and power

Elizabeth Lloyd Mayer

The intersecting import of the two cartoons reproduced on the next pages may, I think, show us, through the unique lens that women's experience gives us, some interesting things about creativity and power at this particular moment in Western culture.

Certainly, there is still plenty to be learned about the general topic of women in relation to creativity and power as joined issues. But beyond that, I think careful attention to how we understand women as they interface with the dual phenomena of creativity and power may help us get a handle on something beyond gender, something important about our larger world and a cultural transition we are facing right now. That transition strikes me as a very exciting one. But it is one that—and this brings us back to the second of the two cartoons—will require some careful consideration if we are to know what has hit us.

One way of summing up our current transition might be to suggest that two crucial insights that psychoanalysis came up with at its inception are starting radically to penetrate the way our larger world is looking at all kinds of things—things ranging from the ways we are starting to understand the nature of material

Your work is surprisingly strong.
Have you always been a woman?

reality, to the nature of consciousness, to the nature of healing; from the world of physics to the world of philosophy. Ultimately, I think these new understandings are going to amount to what is popularly referred to as "a paradigm shift". And, ultimately, I think they stand to alter our views of power and creativity in ways that may be illuminated by looking to women and the ways women experience living in our culture.

The two insights that psychoanalysis gave us hinge on acknowledging the power of love and the power of the unconscious. Psychoanalysis got us thinking about the power of these to create and ultimately transform our experience of being in the world. In laying claim to the transformative power of both those things, psychoanalysis laid the groundwork for a new conceptualization of creativity: what it is and what fuels it. Over time, analysts have done a lot with that conceptualization. In particular, they have done a lot to understand creativity as it manifests in an individual human mind. They have done a lot to understand how the power of love and the power of the unconscious critically determine the nature of an individual's creativity in adapting to life.

But note: I said the creativity of an individual human mind and the ways an individual adapts creatively to the business of living. In fact, for emphasis, I would say that what psychoanalysis has helped us learn most about so far is what I would call creativity in a highly boundaried individual human mind. Psychoanalysis has, ever since Freud, been terrifically focused on the uniqueness of the

ZIPPY, A "PIN-HEAD" CLOWNISH CHARACTER, TRYING TO MAKE SENSE OF THE PHILOSOPHICAL AND EXISTENTIAL CONUNDRUMS OF OUR WORLD—IN SOME WAYS, THE ULTIMATE FREE ASSOCIATER.

individual and the development of things like a sense of self, autonomous ego functions, and the process of separation–individuation as defining the crucial paths to creativity and mature development.

Of course, psychoanalysis has set that boundaried individual human mind within the context of what we call object relations—by which we mean love. But even the term, "object relations", emphasizes the boundaried aspects of how we situate ourselves for love. We—who love—locate ourselves as subject in relation to the beloved—objects. We direct what we have variously called desire or attachment or our instinctual aims towards those objects, most of whom happen to be people. That is how psychoanalysts talk about what happens when we love.

It does not quite evoke the poets—Rumi (1998, p. 50), say:

> Lover and Loving are inseparable and timeless . . .
> My pen breaks and the paper slips away
>   at the ineffable place
> Where Lover, Loving and Loved are one.

Or Phaedo and the early Greeks:

> Love is the divinity who creates peace among men, and calm upon the sea. . . . Love divests us of all alienation from each other, and fills our vacant hearts with overflowing sympathy. . . . Love who showers benignity upon the world, and before whose presence all harsh passions flee and perish . . . the ornament and governor of all things human and divine . . .
>
> ["Agathon Speaks of Love", in Goudge, 1964]

Or Robert Herrick's quatrain:

Thou art my life, my love, my heart,
 The very eyes of me;
And hast command of every part
 To live and die for thee.

["To Anthea Who May Command Him Anything",
in Goudge, 1964]

So why, when psychoanalysts talk about love, does it not sound like Rumi or Phaedo or Herrick—or, for that matter, Dante or Shakespeare or any of the great artists, poets, philosophers, and mystics who have talked about the essence of what it is to love and be loved?

The biggest discrepancy strikes me as our psychoanalytic emphasis on boundedness and separation. As soon as we talk about loving in terms of object ties and object relations, we have put separation and separability at the heart of things. A subject acts whereas an object is acted upon. One is one and the other is the other. The roles, functions, and identities of each are distinct and differentiable: by definition, separate and separable.

So now, back to women. Our emphasis on the importance of relationality for women has begun to re-cast our emphasis on boundaries over the past two decades. We have begun to put Gilligan's (1982) ethic of care centre stage in examining morality. Our thinking about what is mutative in therapeutic work has incorporated much more about relationship, much less about the need for neutrality and separation between persons to achieve the insight and growth that lead to psychic change.

But I would like at this point to ask whether we have gone even close to far enough. Let me go back to Zippy and that second cartoon. Undercutting the centrality of boundaries and separation in defining the nature of the human mind strikes me as what is essential in the paradigm shift our world is facing, the rumblings of which we are just starting to recognize. Those rumblings are likely to have earth-shaking implications for how we think about creativity: what it is, what fuels it, and what blocks it.

And the thing about women in relation to creativity is this. Women's creativity does remain—in our still patriarchal and phallocentric world—marginalized. Being marginalized has a double edge. On the one hand, it's no fun. It leads to feeling disempowered. It leads to feeling homeless. The margins are not where feelings of certainty or security tend to flourish.

On the other hand, the useful thing about living on the margins is the way being outside allows perspective on what is inside. And that may be just what counts when it comes to creativity. Creativity comes from seeing things in new ways. Arthur Koestler, in his *Act of Creation* (1964), described creativity as a sudden juxtaposition of the unexpected. Creativity is what happens when things bang up against each other in ways we never anticipated and something new bursts on the scene as a result.

When you live on the margins, you are always colliding with the unexpected—it is a *sine qua non* of what life at the margins is all about. The key question for women right now is not how to eliminate living at that edge, even with all the anxiety and uncertainty it inevitably breeds. The question instead is how to ride it without fear. The question is how women can learn to embrace it. Because I do believe that the marginal edge is where women's potential for creativity most powerfully resides. It is exactly what the gentleman in my first cartoon did not grasp: the idea that a woman's good work comes precisely out of being a woman, not out of some remarkable facility for having once been (or currently being, or in fantasy someday becoming) a man. Frankly, I anticipate that woman's really good work—her most creative contributions to the world that's just around the corner—will critically hinge on her locating not just comfort but genuine exhilaration in the fact that the familiar male-centred heart of things is exactly where she does not and cannot reside.

However, seeing with a marginal perspective is one thing. Growing that perspective into something that is communicable and recognizable as a creative act in the world is another. The latter requires tremendous clarity of mind, dedication, and hard work, all three of which are hard to develop while living life on the margins. It is hard to forge the tools that carve out a place in the mainstream world while living life on the margins. It is just too isolating.

But that is precisely where women and women's creativity may hook up with the paradigm shift that is still at the edge of awareness for most of us so we can learn something.

Women tend to be cognizant of just how isolating life on the margins is. I am not suggesting that they are comfortable with the isolation—quite the contrary. But they do tend to be comfortable acknowledging the isolation as well as its inhibiting effects. Isolation is all about separation. It is about feeling oneself to be separate, but also about recognizing how that separation feels problematic, how it hurts, and how it registers as quintessentially salient when you look around and assess what matters in the world.

What I have described as the new era in thinking towards which we are heading is a quintessential challenge to the world-view that privileges a sense of separation, identifying it as non-problematic. It is a view that hinges on perceiving connectedness where we have never seen it before—connectedness of all kinds. The readiness to perceive that connectedness strikes me as the critical ingredient that will fuel creativity as we approach the future. Women—precisely because of their awareness of how isolation and separation can inhibit—may be especially primed for access to the version of creativity we will be needing.

Let me go back to Zippy's paradigm shift and locate some ways in which new evidence of connectedness is starting to permeate our thinking in a number of arenas. We are seeing new connections between mind and body as we discover how pain diminishes endocrine and immune function, how fear slows post-operative recovery, how stress delays wound healing, and how mental visualization speeds all varieties of physiologic cure (Dossey, 1999; Pert, 1997). We are seeing an explosion of books from the corporate sphere suggesting new ways in which a pervasive connectedness characterizes the world in which business needs to function (Lipman-Blumen, 1996; Wheatley, 1994). Ellen Berscheid's 1999 Distinguished Scientific Contribution Address to the American Psychological Association heralded "a new science of relationality", based in the recognition that all realms of human endeavour are infused by qualities of interconnectedness we have not previously identified. We have been addressing the import of newly perceived connectedness in the sciences for some time; as far back as 1974, the physicist John Wheeler was suggesting: "We are inescapably involved in bringing about that which appears to be happening. We are not only observers. We are participators. *In some strange sense this is a participatory universe*" (p. 689; emphasis added). The implication of Wheeler's statement for how we view the world is enormous—and for how we view the world creatively, maybe even bigger. (For a more detailed summary of relevant research in a variety of fields, see Mayer, 2000.)

The concept of a genuinely participatory universe makes major demands on us in all kinds of ways. For starters, it makes major demands on scientific methodology as we have known it. It requires that we initiate strategies for investigative methodologies which are themselves participatory, embodying new forms of connectedness between observer and observed. It requires methodologies in which self-awareness on the part of the investigator and a capacity for empathy with that being investigated represent crucial variables in considering the effect of the observer on whatever is constituted as observation (Harman, 1998; Skolimowski, 1994).

To put it bluntly, this strikes me as the science that women have been longing for. It incorporates an approach to knowing that fills out the picture of knowledge that Western culture has been systematically building ever since the Enlightenment. It highlights qualities of discovery making described by investigators like Nobel-prize-winning geneticist Barbara McClintock or cancer researcher June Goodfield. McClintock emphasized the extent to which "a feeling for the organism" enabled her to know each of her corn plants well enough to make her revolutionary discoveries about them. She insisted that original discoveries in science are the product of a profound quality of feeling for whatever is being studied, a degree of empathy usually reserved for intimate human relations. In a moment of uncharacteristic hyperbolae, McClintock once commented: "Every time I walk on grass, I feel sorry because I know the grass is screaming at me" (quoted in Keller, 1983, p. 200). Goodfield put her version of the same thing this way: "If you want to really understand a tumor, you've got to be a tumor" (quoted in Keller, 1983, p. 207).

These are not exactly the descriptions of scientific knowing or scientific methodology to which most of us were educated. To the extent they have been acknowledged at all, they have tended to function on the level of the implicit: background to the way a good scientist needs to think. Rendered explicit, they have a slightly suspicious ring for most of us, conjuring fears of a slippery slope to the irrational just around the corner.

But the states of mind McClintock and Goodfield have highlighted are far from representing a substitute for rationality as we have known it. Nor do they undermine scientific method as we have come to rely on it. They merely describe another dimension of mental functioning that, I would suggest, has remained more private than public in the articulation of scholarly knowledge, but nonetheless underpins all knowing—scientific knowing included.

Carol Gilligan and I recently taught a seminar to women undergraduates at Harvard. We received a large assortment of emails afterwards, most of which described how these young women felt they had to excise certain things from what they said in class and what they wrote in papers. In particular, knowledge that was too "personal", too "subjective", too "focused on feelings", or—most of all—"too much about relationships instead of logic" was not knowledge that counted. They described being painfully aware of how editing that kind of knowledge out of their work was costing them passion, originality, and authenticity—in brief, short-circuiting their creativity. They talked about how their most private knowing stayed out of their public discourse. They were describing their own versions of life at the margins.

The discontent they were expressing certainly does not belong exclusively to women. But I do think looking to women's experience right now may give us a chance to understand the nature of that discontent with particular clarity—because it has a distinctive ubiquity for women in our culture. (And that is not to issue a brief for women's creativity over men's. We've suffered too many years of psychoanalytic history in which discussions of gender difference reduce to argument over which is better. We do not need more of that.)

What I am suggesting is that we highlight the value of turning life at the margins—women's or anyone else's—into the capacity for distinctively original forms of creativity rather than allowing it to sink into the experience of lack. The real act of empowerment for women will not come out of finally locating the male-centred mainstream as home. It will come instead out of claiming the profound value of women's history just as it has been and the equally profound value of women's identity just as it is. In that sense, laying claim to disempowerment constitutes a uniquely powerful form of power, an act of acceptance that permits precisely those acts of creation that might prove potently and imaginatively new.

Finally, let me return to our psychoanalytic beginnings: to the power of love and the power of the unconscious. Just as those two things have been key to psychoanalytic discovery from its inception, I believe that they will end up key in the era of discovery that lies ahead. As we integrate a new grasp of how connectedness is at the heart of all kinds of things, I think we will be expanding our understanding of love and our understanding of unconscious mental processes in ways we have barely anticipated.

I think we will find that taking radically extended account of the ways connectedness functions in love will transform not just the ways we go about investigating and comprehending the world, but also how we actually live in it. It will make love a critical variable in arenas we have exempted from love's purview—along the lines, for example, suggested by McClintock in scientific investigation. And taking radically extended account of the ways connectedness functions in the unconscious will have us looking not just to individual minds—to ways, for example, in which one individual's thoughts and feelings connect, or ways a single individual's manifest and latent ideas connect, or ways a person's motivations and behaviour connect. It will have us also glimpsing previously unrecognized ways in which unconscious connections between minds—between individuals—determine what we know, how we know, and the vastly complex fields within which we affect each other.

I anticipate, then, that we will be looking in two directions as we aim to spark creativity in the era that lies ahead. On the one hand, we will be looking to an extended picture of what psychoanalysis can show us about the power of love and the power of the unconscious. On the other, we will be looking to women and to those margins where women have lived as they have gone about the ordinary business of living as women. Inside that ordinary business may reside potent clues to grasping how our existence is informed by a vastly more connected universe than we have considered to date. Perhaps it is time to lift those clues from the often-inchoate, still-too-private domain of women's experience into the outright centre of our efforts to illuminate the radical cast that power and creativity will have in the world that is around the corner.

CHAPTER SEVEN

Character and creativity

Elisabeth Young-Bruehl

In his essay on Edgar Allan Poe, the poet Charles Baudelaire (1981) offered a general reflection on the importance of adolescence in the development of character, genius, and style:

> All those who have reflected upon their own lives, who have often looked back in order to compare their past with their present, all those who have acquired the habit of self-analysis know what an immense part adolescence plays in the ultimate nature of a man. It is then that objects deeply implant their imprint on tender, pliant minds: it is then that colors are gaudy and that the senses speak a mysterious language. The character, the genius, the style of a man are formed by seemingly common circumstances of his early youth. If all the men who have occupied the world's stage had noted their childhood impressions, what an excellent psychological dictionary we would possess! [p. 14]

Baudelaire, it seems to me, underestimated the psychological dictionary that exists in the works of men and women who have come upon the world's stage as creators, as originators of works of art. This dictionary is little read, however, because a guide for its use, a guide to how character, genius, and style—to use Baudelaire's terms—define each other, has not been developed.

I think that such a guide could be built up with the help of a notion I call "the character-ideal". My idea is that in their late adolescences creative people form for themselves—sometimes consciously, but usually unconsciously—a guiding image of the character they wish for, the sort of genius that will be able to subtend, to be the origin for, their style, their creativity. This guiding image or character-ideal is formed on the basis of the character an adolescent has: it is an idealization of an existing state of psychic affairs, a projection on the basis of a developmental history.

Sigmund Freud offered the very rich idea that people form images of ideal societies—utopias—and of natural processes and orders on the basis of their internal perceptions of themselves. He called these images "endopsychic perceptions." His idea was that people project outward their crucial developmental icon—the story of their Oedipus complex—and he assumed that they idealized this story in the projecting: that is, that they projected not how things had truly been oedipally with them, but how they wished things had been—and still were. They projected what he called "the family romance" (1909c). So, we find our traditions full of societal stories about magnificent Founding Fathers and natural historical stories about the cosmos having been commanded into being by a Creator Father or a divine Demiurge, and so forth. Religions and philosophies are, in sum, psychic stories, family romance fantasies, turned outward and writ very large.

I find this idea of Freud's very rich, if rather too focused on oedipal desires and too patriarchal to compass, say, Mother Earth images, but I want to add something to the idea. It seems to me that adolescents, at one remove of libidinal development from the "sexual efflorescence" (as Freud, 1923a [1922], called it) of the oedipal period, tend to have "endopsychic perceptions" of another kind than children have. They perceive themselves, their psychic apparatuses, in terms of how they are, or are not, ordered. In the upheaval of adolescence, they long for order, for an independent New World of psychic order, to which psychoanalysis has, since Erik Erikson's work (1950), given the name "identity".

This adolescent image of mind–body order, this "character-ideal", is, I think apparent in creative works of all sorts—literary, philosophical, visual, musical, and so forth. It is the origin, as Freud (1927c) noted, for projections of the ideal society and images of the cosmos. But I think it is also the origin for creative people's images of creativity: it determines the way they imagine creative processes, their own and others'. Theories of creativity are expressions of "endopsychic perception" of creativity in action. This is, by the way, the reason why—I think—the search perennially conducted by psychoanalysts for *the* key to creativity, *the* creative process, is a perfectly futile and misconceived search, as is the recent feminist search for *the* creativity specific to females. There are creative processes, in the plural, and these stem from different creative characterological types, which are not specific to the two sexes, though they may have particular differences that are sex- or gender-specific.

* * *

It is on the basis of biographical study that I have come to the conclusion—a hypothetical one—that there are basically three different kinds of "character-ideals" or images of ideal psychic order developed by adolescents in the course of their identity quests. What I would like to do here is to sketch in very summary terms these three types and then offer biographical illustrations of one of them.

1. The first type is an image of wild forces brought under control by a commanding figure, a figure of such charisma that it can over time, evolutionarily, bring about order without violence, by sheer force of will or personality or authority.

In the history of psychological inquiries into the nature and processes of creativity, it is Sigmund Freud who has most persuasively made this type of character-ideal the centrepiece of his theory. Freud argued that creative work depends on a person's ability to sublimate—to channel and dedicate libidinal forces, the wild reservoir of the id, to cultural purposes. Freud portrayed the creator as a person of strong, charismatic ego, a person who, as he first said in his biographical essay on Leonardo da Vinci (Freud,

1910c) and reiterated in the late small essay called "Libidinal Types" (1931a) works from a narcissistic characterological base.

2. The second type of image of ideal psychic order, or character-ideal, features a figure who works upon matter that needs shaping, moulding, forming. This image is artisanal: a well-ordered self is a self in which one part has been able to make the other part beautiful. Such people are following Oscar Wilde's well-known advice: "Create yourself! Be yourself your poem." And this injunction can be glossed by turning to Richard Ellmann (1987), Oscar Wilde's most sophisticated biographer, who noted that in general the greatness of the Wildean hero can be measured by the degree to which he transforms the actual substance of his life. Whenever he permits his own passions to be seen, they are ignoble distraction. These unpleasant realities are irrelevant to the artistic production. Wilde did not imagine character as a channelling of forces of libidinal disposition or natural temperament; he imagined character as replacing nature, and he exalted the completely artificial self.

In some creative people of this character-ideal sort, the fabricating image is, however, one of reproduction rather than production. These people imagine the psyche as having two parts, one male and one female, which together make a "child of the soul" (as Plato called the poet's work). Women of this character type, not surprisingly, tend to imagine themselves as reproducers more frequently than do men, but production images and reproduction images are not gender-specific.

Theories of creativity generated by people of this second creative characterological type take two general forms according to whether the emphasis is on production or reproduction. If the emphasis is on production, these theories of creativity present images of the self splitting and then reuniting through a moulding or sculpting process. The split-off moulder or sculptor is very often presented as an impostor, or a poseur, a figure who can assume many guises and then bring the material or to-be-formed part into accord with those guises. If the emphasis is on reproduction, the bisexuality or androgyny or hermaphroditism of the psyche is emphasized and celebrated—as bisexuality or homosexuality in object choice is often practised. Males often speak of themselves, as Friedrich Nietzsche did, as "male mothers", and they sing the praises of the female's capacity for giving birth. Females analogize their creativity to their procreativity but imagine that they have in themselves a paternal, inseminating figure (who is very often modelled on their father). In theories of this sort, inspiration plays a large role—and it is conceived of as an ability either to inseminate or be inseminated. Not sublimation, but splitting is the key creative mechanism for people of this sort.

3. The third type of image of ideal psychic order or character-ideal is one in which a true self, a pure or uncorrupted self, throws off or strips itself of all impurities, all mere matter, all corruptible flesh, all shackles that keep it from creative flight or prevent its salvation. This is the image fundamental to all who conceive of order as arising from spiritual discipline, achievement of undistracted attention or concentration, and, usually, sexual abstinence or at least some very regulated form of asceticism or so-called Platonic love.

Creativity, according to people of this third sort, has more to do with a state of mind than an actual product or achievement in the world. Worldly products are, at most, a record of a process of transcending the world, escaping its corruptions, finding peace, serenity, purity—though worldly products may be very highly valued for their pedagogical or exemplary force, their status as manuals of salvation or prevention of illness. Spiritual exercises, meditation, or periods of self-humbling and self-denial are typical of this Stoic or, one might even say, Buddhistic modality. The libidinal organization or character type that is the basis for this type of creativity and theorizing about creativity is, usually, the character that Freud called "anal", which is known diagnostically as "the obsessional character".

* * *

What I have noted about these three kinds of character-ideals is very condensed and abbreviated, and I think it will make more sense with an illustration. There is not space to illustrate all three types, so I shall chose the third one—the self-stripping or self-transcending ascetic character-ideal type—and offer little sketches of a quartet of female exemplars who shared neither genre nor historical period nor native tongue.

Let me begin by noting that people with character-ideals of the third type speak as T. S. Eliot did in *The Use of Poetry and the Use of Criticism* (1933) about what inspiration feels like:

> a disturbance of our quotidian character which results in an incantation, an outburst of words which we hardly recognize as our own (because of the effortlessness. . . . [To] me, it seems that at these moments, which are characterized by the sudden lifting of the burden of anxiety and fear which press upon our daily life so steadily that we are unaware of it, what happens is something negative: that is to say, not "inspiration" as we commonly think of it, but the breaking down of strong habitual barriers—which tend to reform very quickly. Some obstruction is momentarily whisked away. The accompanying feeling is less like what we know as a positive pleasure, than a sudden relief from an intolerable burden. [pp. 144–145]

Disburdening—or what I have called self-stripping—is the action of the ascetic or spiritual character-ideal. Stoical or sexually overstrict religious traditionalists of Eliot's sort often project such an ideal. But stripping the self of all its accidentality or materiality, revealing the essential self in its purity, can serve many purposes, and not the least among them is escape from psychic and social conditions in which being female seems a limitation, an inadequacy.

In her biography of the French philosopher Simone Weil, Simone Pétrement (1976) described her subject as a *lycée* student:

> As for the plans she had already formed, her whole conception of what she wanted to do with her life, it was—as she herself later said—a great misfortune to have been born female. So she decided to reduce this obstacle as much as possible by disregarding it, that is, by giving up any desire to think of herself as a woman or to be regarded as such by others. . . . Her parents called her "Simon," "our son number two," and "our *cagne* boy." When Simone wrote to her mother while at Henri IV [her *lycée*], she even went so far as to speak of herself in the masculine gender and to sign her letters "your respectful son." [p. 27]

Simone Weil gave up her femininity for the gender she regarded as generic: she joined, as it were, mankind.

But her project also had quite specific purpose within her family context, in the shadow of her astoundingly precocious mathematician brother Andrew and in the atmosphere of her mother's contempt for feminine frailties and silliness. In her "Spiritual Autobiography", Weil (1977) recalled that:

> At fourteen I fell into one of those fits of bottomless despair that come with adolescence, and I seriously thought of dying because of the mediocrity of my natural faculties. The exceptional gifts of my brother, who had a childhood and youth comparable to those of Pascal, brought my own inferiority home to me. I did not mind having no visible successes, but what did grieve me was the idea of being excluded from that transcendent kingdom to which only the truly great have access and wherein truth abides. I prepared to die rather than to live without that truth. After months of inward darkness, I suddenly had the everlasting conviction that any human being, even though practically devoid of natural faculties, can penetrate to the kingdom of truth reserved for genius, if only he longs for truth and perpetually concentrates all his attention upon its attainment. He thus becomes a genius, too, even though for lack of talent his genius cannot be visible from the outside. Later on, when the strain of headaches caused the feeble faculties I possess to be invaded by a paralysis, which I was quick to imagine as probably incurable, the same conviction led me to persevere for ten years in an effort of concentrated attention that was practically unsupported by any hope of results. [p. 91]

The sibling rivalry, the competition for prowess as a penetrator into a romanticized kingdom of truth, the stress on her own "invisible" equipment, give this passage all the marks of the Freudianly defined "masculinity complex", but what is important in the context I am developing is Simone Weil's solution: paring herself down to an ascetic, rarefied attentiveness. The purity does not come, as with Oscar Wilde, from self-shaping—rarefaction or transformation by constant reworking—but by elimination, purgation. It is no psychic accident that Simone Weil later ended her life in a martyrdom that took the form of self-starvation, anorexia.

A person of this character-ideal type might also describe her life and her writing style with words like these:

> I try to eliminate what isn't essential, and I try not to give in, as I did in my youth, to the temptation to add ornament. Back then I thought it was necessary to round off each sentence. Now I look instead for the sharpest possible sentence, the simplest images, and I don't try to be original at all costs. In fact, I don't try anything at all; my writing is the way it is. [Yourcenar, 1984a, p. 185]

This woman, cited from a collection of her interviews appropriately titled *With Open Eyes*, is the Belgian-born novelist Marguerite Yourcenar, the first woman ever to be initiated into the Académie Française. She was speaking of the style she had first worked for in *Alexis* (1984b), a *recit* or monologue penned by a young man explaining to his wife that he is a homosexual and cannot continue in their marriage. Yourcenar published the book when she was 26, in 1929. Later she declared that she hoped to be like the central character in her novel *The Abyss* (1976), Zeno, who is a mystic pursing a goal typical of the self-purifier: to "die a little less besotted than he was born".

Near the end of her life, at the age of 83, Yourcenar told an interviewer about the character-ideal she had since her youth—even before she produced a collection of male literary characters to present the ideal, and before she had achieved a lean, graceful prose style to announce it.

> Yourcenar: ". . . I don't mean to say that I will be fundamentally different—whatever I am I have probably been all my life—but I shall at least have gotten rid of a lot of excess baggage, or so I hope."
>
> Interviewer: "For you, then, life is primarily a matter of divestiture."
>
> Yourcenar: "Yes, certainly, but it is also a matter of enrichment. One sheds one's clothing in order to be bronzed by the sun's rays." [1984a, pp. 254–255]

For Yourcenar, the spiritual discipline that lets an individual being (*un être*) understand that he or she is an essence (*l'être*) was a matter of course in much of the ancient world, in the Stoic quarters of Greece and Rome that she knew well as an amateur classicist, and also in the East.

> Generally speaking, one must try against considerable difficulty to achieve what Hindu sages describe as a state of "attentiveness," in which you get rid of three-quarters or nine-tenths of what you seem to think but really don't. Ordinarily, a person merely assembles bits and pieces of pre-existing ideas. All these must be eliminated and one's thought focused on nothing; the effect is quite salutary. [1984a, p. 119]

In Marguerite Yourcenar's social vision, all human particularities and differences were eventually to be overcome. Men and women would know themselves as humans; homosexuality and heterosexuality would become, simply, expressions of sexuality; people would come to respect animals and plants as fellow creatures, citizens of one world. The corollary to Marguerite Yourcenar's cosmopolitanism is a spiritual feeling for the cosmos that is almost pantheistic.

In comparison to Simone Weil and Marguerite Yourcenar, Gertrude Stein, who was born in 1874, some twenty-five years before the French-speaking contemporaries, conceived of the process of stripping the self down to its essentials in temporal rather than spatial terms. She eliminated past and future and focused her attention only on the present. Having encountered William James's characterology when she was a student at Radcliffe, she concluded that every individual has a character—she called it "the bottom nature" (1937, p. 266)—that never varies, which means that the present is the past being repeated and the future is what the present will be when it repeats itself. In her dualistic characterology, people are either of the "independent dependent kind" or of the "dependent independent kind", and the words and deeds of people within these two types are endlessly, infinitely repeated. Or, as she said of the book called *Three Lives,* in which she first embodied her vision of psychic order:

> In that there was a constant recurring and beginning there was a marked direction in the direction of being in the present although naturally I had been accustomed to past present future, and why, because the composition formation around me was a prolonged present. [1998, p. 524]

The literary language for expressing this temporal a-linearity or amorphousness was to be a language, she concluded, stripped of sentence structure and burdensome rules: "The question is, if you have a vocabulary have you any need of grammar?" (Stein, 1973).

In Gertrude Stein's image of psychic order there was also—not surprisingly—no structure, no division; she completely rejected Freud's theory of the unconscious. As she firmly said of herself (in the third person singular, writing the *Autobiography of Alice B. Toklas*): "Gertrude Stein never had subconscious reactions ..." (1990, p. 79). Similarly, she claimed that there are no differences between people who want no differences between them: she insisted as she wrote Alice B. Toklas's autobiography that she and her friend were one, and then she went right on to insist that she could write the autobiography of America—a book called "*The Making of the Americans*"—or even "*Everybody's Autobiography*". Her social vision was an expanded version of her character-ideal, which was an ideal of a singular psyche, without fixed order, stratification, structuration, or differentiation.

Stripping the self down to essentials, purifying it, can be accomplished in spirits as different as Simone Weil's—self-castigation or rebuke—and Marguerite Yourcenar's—ecstatic nature worship—and Gertrude Stein's—self-congratulation. It can also be undertaken for quite different purposes, by quite different psychic means. Anna Freud offered a classic description of one such means in a quite autobiographical passage on "altruistic surrender" in her 1936 book *The Ego and the Mechanisms of Defence*. Altruistic surrender, which is a means of stripping the self of forbidden wishes by making over the wishes to others, can also translate easily enough into a social vision, as Anna Freud herself noted during an informal discussion of her idea that was recorded in *Analysis of Defence* (Sandler, 1985):

> If you can't get what you want yourself and enjoy it yourself because it's prohibited by internal conflict, well at least somebody else can get it, and you can enjoy it there through what you call vicarious enjoyment—which is certainly worth while. But that isn't all. At the same time the process liberates, or creates an outlet for aggression. What I meant was that originally the individual wants to pursue his or her instinctual aims aggressively. "I want it, I'll have it, I'll fight anybody who

> won't give it to me." This aggression becomes impossible and forbidden when the fulfillment of the wish becomes impossible and forbidden, but now with the altruism you can fight for somebody else's fulfillment of the wish with the same aggression, the same energy. So you have both your libidinal vicarious pleasure, and you have an outlet for your aggression. It's surprising that not more people are altruists! [pp. 451–452]

Many democratic and anarchistic social visionaries, of course, have conjured a harmonious world in which there would be no divisions among masterful leaders and followers, people-shapers and people-shaped, in which all people would do unto others as they wish others would do unto them, or in which each would get according to his or her needs. But Anna Freud was able to imagine what non-hierarchical social harmony would actually require psychologically—that is, that all people find appropriate others whom they can help to do what they once wished to do for themselves but could not. In such a world, there would not be philanthropists and recipients of philanthropy, do-gooders and possibly quite resentful gooders-done-to—another form of hierarchy—but rather altruism that would be as universal as the universality of forbidden wishes. Each person would give according to his or her psychological need, and each would get an outlet for forbidden wishes and aggression.

* * *

It really is surprising that not more people are altruists! But, then, if it is the case that, as I have been arguing, people can only be creative in the modes that their characters permit and promote, we would all do better for ourselves and for others to celebrate our diversity than to try—unless we are characterogically suited for it—to redistribute our aggression. In the multicultural spirit of the moment—so welcome—we would do well to celebrate multi-characterism.

But, in closing, I want to remark one further consequence of this characterological approach to creativity. If it is the case, as I believe it is, that people are able to be creative only when they are going with and growing with their characters, and not opposing them or trying to do things that they do not permit or working in situations or contexts that do not support their characters, then one of the keys to creativity for any individual woman is to be able to understand and identify her character and work to secure for herself the conditions and relationships that permit it to flourish. The phrase "strength of character" is well known and so well used that it is clichéd, but I am suggesting that there are ways to explore and develop strength of character that serve creativity—and one of these is psychoanalytic description.

THE PHALLUS
Point/counterpoint

CHAPTER EIGHT

Feminine influence and power

Alcira Mariam Alizade

In this chapter, I present my concept of feminine influence or feminine power and its potential social effects. There is a very extensive literature on power, which I will not attempt to summarize. Rather, I wish to suggest a direction to take in exploration of feminine power.

First, let us begin to define feminine power. It is a paradoxical power, a kind of inner strength and ethical value that has developed very slowly and over many centuries. This form of power depends on femininity for its existence. It displaces conventional ideas of masculine power. Feminine power has required a long process of learning to develop.

The word "power" is familiar to all, but it refers to a variety of meanings and has changed throughout history. Michel Foucault (1976) emphasizes that power is not an institution or a structure and is also not a kind of potential within some individuals. Rather, it is the name we give to a complex strategic situation in a particular society. Power is everywhere and comes from everywhere (Foucault, 1976, p. 113). The locus of power shifts constantly. It resides within every organization, manifesting as organizational control. Each form of power has its individual laws and rules, and each act of dominance is an exercise of power. Power is exerted in various ways by different people and institutions, but it is essential to the functioning of organized societies in order to tame violence.

There are both positive and negative aspects of power. From a psychological point of view, positive aspects of power are closely linked to self-mastery and autonomy. Such manifestations of power sometimes emerge late in life, as a result of maturity. One example is power over oneself, which may be termed an everyday power. Leadership and obedience to the authority of rules and laws constitute other constructive qualities of power.

Negative aspects of power involve the expression of excessive selfishness, unbounded self-love (Freud, 1919h, p. 242), and sadistic pleasure. In the damaging egoism found in pathological narcissism, the fellow-being—whether he is a son, a parent, or a friend—is ignored. Cruelty in human communication, even if disguised in human communication, is another negative manifestation of power. In cruelty, the moral motives of human love are destroyed. A hidden monster emerging from within the exercise of cruel narcissistic power may lead to striving for, and even achieving, absolute power. This striving after unlimited power can result in tyranny and genocide.

Psychological origins of the need for power

Let us first examine some of Freud's concepts that relate to the origin of the need for power. The concept of primary helplessness (Freud, 1950 [1985]) is a useful beginning. In his words,

> At first, the human organism is incapable of bringing about the specific action. It takes place by extraneous help, when the attention of an experienced person is drawn to the child's state by discharge along the path of internal change. In this way this path of discharge acquires a secondary function of the highest importance, that of communication, and the initial helplessness of human beings is the primal source of all moral motives.

> When the helpful person has performed the work of the specific action in the external world for the helpless one. [1950 (1985), pp. 318–319]

These words emphasize the human being's original vulnerability and helplessness. When brought into the world as newborns, we all are completely vulnerable. It is vital, in order to survive, to have a helpful person next to us. The helpful adult automatically exerts power over the infant. Our primary helplessness provides an early lesson in the importance of helping and being helped. Ethical values favouring helping in later social life originate in this early state, but also the helplessness of the infant in the hands of the caregiver suggests primal ways of increasing one's domination over a helpless person by encouraging helplessness.

I turn next to Freud's ideas of the narcissistic wound (Freud, 1914c) and denial of mortality (1919h, p. 242):

> At the most touchy point in the narcissistic system, the immortality of the ego, which is so hard pressed by reality. . . . "All men are mortal" is paraded in text-books of logic as an example of a general proposition; but no human being really grasps it, and our unconscious has as little use now as ever for the idea of its own mortality. [1914c, p. 91]

Grandiosity is almost unavoidable in people who have achieved great power. It is easy for them to fall under the illusion of possessing unlimited power and being surrounded by an eternal triumphant environment. It is based on a phallic, omnipotent fantasy.

However, even the powerful may suffer from "godlike discontent" (Freud, 1930a):

> Man has, as it were, become a kind of prosthetic God when he puts on all his auxiliary organs he is truly magnificent, but those organs have not grown on to him and they still give him much trouble at times. . . . In the interest of our investigations, we will not forget that present-day man does not feel happy in his Godlike character. [1930a, p. 91]

Denial of human limitations in gaining and exercising power can involve the fantasy of reaching the status of a god. However, satisfaction of this fantasy can never be fulfilled. The impossibility of reaching such grandiose ideal goals may result in depression, psychosomatic disorders, and a general sense of discontent.

Having a child to whom can be delegated the primal illusion of being a godlike little person, "His (or her) Majesty the Baby" (Freud, 1930a, p. 91), may calm adult castration anxieties and the sense of painful limitations. Thus, the painful knowledge of the impermanent human condition can be temporarily suppressed, and, once more, the fantasy of being like the gods, powerful and imperishable, is partly gratified. This wishful fantasy involves a denial of mortality, transiently possible in identification with the infant whose vulnerability is repressed, letting the intensely grandiose ideal image of oneself as a powerful and immortal baby-king emerge.

It is very important to remember that human beings have murderous instincts. As Freud (1915) has told us, all human beings are potential assassins. He reminds us that, "there is no instinctive rejection to blood shedding. We descend from an innumerable offspring of assassins. The will to kill is in our blood" (Freud, 1930a, p. 242). In the presence of severe narcissistic disturbances, destructive impulses predominate and phallic unlimited power is sought. Killing a human being expresses the desire for mastery over life and death, absolute power. For primitive minds, the act of killing another person, directly or indirectly commanding a murder, produces an exciting conviction of having absolute power. This tumescent phallic satisfaction can, in such individuals, override the sense of reality. Such expression of destructive power is accompanied by the unbounded selfishness and sadistic pleasure of the potential assassin. In these pathological situations, power becomes a refuge disguising biological dependence and mortality. It is employed to calm death anxieties and compensate for the primary helplessness.

I now turn to Freud's ideas about the repudiation of femininity (cf. Alizade, 1993) and the relationship of this concept to that of power, particularly feminine power.

> Both in the therapeutic and in character-analyses we notice that two themes come into especial prominence ... the two themes are tied to the distinction between the sexes; one is a characteristic of males as the other is of females. In spite of the dissimilarity of their content, there is an obvious correspond-

> ence between them. . . . The two corresponding themes are, in the female, an envy for the penis—a positive striving to possess a male genital—and, in the male, a struggle against his passive or feminine attitude to another male. What is common to the two themes was singled out at an early date by psychoanalytic nomenclature as an attitude towards the castration complex. Subsequently Alfred Adler brought the term "masculine protest" into current use. It fits the case of males perfectly; but I think that, from the start, "repudiation of femininity" would have been the correct description of this remarkable feature in the psychical life of human beings. [Freud, 1937c, p. 250]

Both men and women repudiate femininity because femininity is associated with weakness and helplessness. This human bedrock is equal for both genders. Men manifest this repudiation openly, while women tend to occupy themselves in acquiring men's characteristics. Penis envy implies keeping a distance from femininity. This repudiation of femininity can be found to some extent in every human being.

All human beings are threatened by fears of insignificance and incompleteness and by fears of reality. We are all merely passers-by. During our voyage through the world, we need some sort of narcissistic satisfaction so we may feel that our names will not disappear after our deaths, that we will leave a mark on civilization. At least, we hope to continue on in the minds of our descendants.

Feminine power—the power of femininity

> "Because I know I shall not know
> The one veritable transitory power."
>
> T. S. Eliot, *Ash-Wednesday*

Two questions must be raised in regard to feminine power: what does feminine power or feminine influence consist of, and from where does feminine power stem? Also, the power of femininity should be differentiated from women's power. Women's power, or the power of any individual woman, is not necessarily based on femininity. In fact, the power of women can be phallic and even evil. This is the case with phallic mothers and perversion in women. Women can and do exert destructive power, although less frequently than men. As I mentioned at the beginning of this chapter, feminine power is a paradoxical power. It may be exerted by women and also by men, in which case it is drawn from their feminine psychic potential. It may also be called feminine influence or feminine authority. This feminine power is both feminine and maternal and is a kind of "non-powered" power. It is an invisible and simultaneously active form of power that steadily influences society and is likely to gain strength in future centuries.

It is not easy to understand this full conceptualization of feminine power, because it is outside more conventional ideas of power, which are based on phallic omnipotent power. Feminine power requires a form of acceptance of castration and the will of mothering humankind. Feminine power accepts and deals with insignificance. Its vital energy is based on life instincts. Women do not develop the will for power in the same way that men do. Therefore, this feminine kind of power can be employed to neutralize more destructive forms of power. It is to be hoped that the expression of feminine power will lead to feminization of culture and political life.

Feminine power has developed slowly. It has developed through a process of learning from the submission, obedience, and the reclusion of women in private life, going back through thousands of years. Women became familiarized with submission, and most lived their whole lives in submission to patriarchal power, shaped by society to dedicate themselves to a household life. They did not possess any political power. They did not hold positions in the armed forces or religious organizations. The structure of society made women become used to obedience and servitude.

Now, let me stress *the positive aspects of servitude.* These words may sound strange. We are accustomed to speaking of submission and servitude in a negative sense.

While we all agree that women have suffered from male domination, revenge and furious rage are counterproductive. They are an obstacle to the development of constructive feminine power. Servitude leads to humility, an acceptance of limitations, as well as symbolic castration. It involves getting closely acquainted with the non–powered world. Helplessness can become an extraordinary teacher. What is learned has biological, physiological, psychological, and sociological sources. *Feminine power is based on femininity and long-term experiences of vulnerability.*

Biological and psychological sources of feminine power

Blood and fluids

Blood and other bodily fluids form one of the sources of feminine power. While men shed blood only when wounded—for example, during war or hunting—women have a natural relationship to blood through their experiences of menstruations, loss of virginity, abortion, delivery, menopause, and so forth. The fluid world that surrounds them speaks of body experiences and deep contact with carnal periodical loss. Bodily fluids stimulate fantasies in both genders. The importance of blood in women and its psychological consequences has not been sufficiently emphasized (Alizade, 1993). This sacred and diabolic substance combined with woman's lack of a penis and the mystery of pregnancy and delivery gave rise to fears of women in primitive minds and resulted in denigration, omnipotent images, repudiation, menstruation taboos, and the like.

The whole problem of sexual differences became oversimplified into having or not having a penis. This dichotomy establishes the first difference between sexes, but it is not the only one. Freud (1924d) stated that "anatomy is destiny" (p. 178). I wish to add that biological transformations establish new fantasied destinies. For example, puberty and menarche reveal a second difference, between those who have a periodical blood flow and those who do not. This difference, having or not having menstruations, is established by blood. It is the source of fantasy and symbolization.

Menstruation in women has been used as an example of natural feminine weakness, as a reason that women should not study, nor work. Menstruation was misperceived as an illness that made women unfit for social functions. It was used to confirm that women's life should be restricted to the privacy of their homes. In this privacy, the feminine imaginary universe became inhabited by fluids: blood and the flow of milk. These liquid substances produced mixed feelings of fascination, fear, and rejection.

Women's bodies are constructed in such a way that they constantly have to deal with fantasized losses. The lack of penis, menstruation, miscarriage, separation from the baby they carry in their wombs—all can represent loss. Some women also feel empty after having had sex, having lost the partner's penis, which can also represent a baby. Thus, women's flesh evokes castration. Through bodily experiences, woman's flesh becomes a kind of natural teacher of material reality, the human condition.

Maternal functions

Pregnancy is the experience of two beings in one body. The mystery of human creation is incarnated in the pregnant woman. The pregnant belly has many meanings. It gives life, but also death in miscarriage or abortion. There is pain, sometimes a dead foetus, and a dying mother. To become pregnant is to risk one's life. Women must accept that they are endangered due to natural physiological laws when they give birth to their babies. In the last century, to die during delivery was common. Women had many children and were exposed to the mortal risk of multiple pregnancies. Men became widowers and did not hesitate to marry younger women who could bear more children and take care of the children from their husband's previous marriages. Spouses were easily replaced (Gay, 1984, p. 221). Women were considered weak, and femininity was repudiated.

Mothering requires time and effort. It can be fun and also a burden. Each "inside story" (Raphael-Leff, 1993) of pregnancy will have a wide range of different issues. Mothering teaches women to offer themselves to their fellow-being, the baby, and can precede future social mothering.

Woman's body, unlike man's, is open. By the open body we understand a body that can be easily penetrated. The vagina is a virtual cavity. One of its main characteristics is its permeability . Blood, babies, penises, and foetuses, all pass through the vagina.

The major danger in having a vagina lies in being easily raped. There is no way to close the body in order to hinder the sexual attack. In addition, the incapacity that some women show in defending themselves from a man's attack is due not only to men's superior muscular strength but also to the woman's learned submission. This submission impedes many women, even if they are strong, from defending themselves.

Psychological and sociological sources

The psychological vulnerability found in a certain group of women is related to the ways in which they are educated and socialized. Dependence and lack of individualism has been fostered, resulting in the production of infantile women who enact a kind of hysterical drama. Speaking like little girls, they simulate being childish and beautifully ignorant. Their cultivated helplessness keeps them at the centre of attention.

Women bear a special cultural signifier: "no". This "no" is tied up with woman's being: that is, not being male and having—that is, not having—a penis. A human being born under the sign "no" will necessarily be located within the imaginary and symbolic dynamics of castration. The "no" devalues the feminine image, contributing powerfully to the social imagination of women's nothingness.

The penis, from the perspective of the cultural, is a phallic symbol. Behind the phallus and beyond it is nothingness, the void, the silence of what is not known, an order outside the influence of phallic power. The imaginary dimension of the nothingness of a woman's body gives birth to fantasies. Women can sometimes represent the incarnation of the mystery of human creation (Alizade, 1999). To incarnate this mystery opens up a dimension of power beyond our current knowledge. It has helped women to regard themselves as strange creatures devoted to the family, beyond the need of public narcissistic fulfilments.

From present to future: hope for the coming centuries

It is to be hoped that the increase of feminine power in cultures will lead to a "feminization" of culture. By feminization of culture, I mean a social movement that leads to a larger amount of influence of femininity on society and civilization. This cultural feminization will foster taming of violent aspects of human nature and enhance social mothering. As a further result of feminization, one can expect there to be narcissistic transformations, ethical progression, and an improvement of societal mental health. Humankind will increase the acceptance of symbolic castration, and the resulting feminization effects will favourably influence education, medical care, and poverty. It is to be hoped that cultural feminization will contribute to the taming of the violent aspects of human nature, and that our inner assassin may be repressed in our deepest unconscious.

Social mothering is akin to biological mothering, but in social mothering the maternal functions take place outside the closed circle of the family. Love allows passing beyond the narcissistic limits of what belongs to me and expands itself into the wide world inhabited by millions of sons and daughters. The person—be it man or woman—who exercises social mothering works towards the building of a huge human family.

"Narcissistic transformation" (Alizade, 1995) involves a change in the structure of the psychic apparatus. It implies a re-ordering of the narcissistic system starting with the decentralization of the subject. This mental change establishes what I call "tertiary narcissism", which brings the subject nearer to acceptance of the perishability of his human condition. Narcissism is projected on to the external world. This libido does not come back to the ego but puts itself to work in the community in order to take care not only of the loving ones, but of the distant human beings one never will get to know. This caring for the "distant object", as I call it, is a psychic process that benefits both the individual person and society. The more a person has transformed his narcissism, the more protected he or she is from the traps of self-idealization.

I want to finish this chapter by leaving some unanswered questions. However, first I shall quote some words expressed by men, related to femininity, power, and ethics.

> Perhaps the dawn of a new ethic is breaking, when man will have sufficiently freed himself from his homosexuality and narcissism, and then, more than the blood of the wounded or dead man, it will be the blood of the living woman which expresses the reality of sex. [Paul Mathis, 1974, p. 147]

> From my experience I conclude that women are superior. Superior physically, more sensible, more capable of loving. I think women should govern and the world would be much better. Those women who have already governed looked more like men in skirts than women themselves: think of Thatcher or Golda Meir. I am speaking of women who will govern from their femininity. [Vittorio Gassmann, 1996]

* * *

My final questions are:

1. Is power the same to a woman as to a man?
2. Will women change our idea of power?
3. Is feminine power really a power?
4. How will feminine power affect political life?
5. Will the outcome be different if women govern the world, or influence men significantly?
6. Men had until now the leadership of historical horror. Will women be as destructive as men once they attain real power?
7. Is feminization of culture a utopia, or may it become real to its full extent?

It is my hope that this chapter will raise questions about women and feminine power, increase our knowledge about power and women, and give birth to future research.

CHAPTER NINE

Looking at women: what do men see?

Robert Alan Glick

In this chapter, I offer a view of women and power from the perspective of the psychology of men—that is, what men see when looking at women. Being quite mindful of the twin dangers over generalization and over abstractness in discussion of this sort, I seek to join the discourse, which appropriately emphasizes powerlessness and disempowerment experienced by women in gender struggles, with the following suggestion: while women tend to see themselves as relatively powerless in relation to men, men, in deep and disturbing ways, do not readily share this view.

What is often insufficiently recognized and acknowledged by both genders is the profound influence that the fear of women holds in shaping the more public perception of women's relative vulnerability and weakness.

Before going further, I wish to issue a disclaimer or two. My views are based on my experience as a psychoanalyst and as a man, not as a social scientist, historian, or cultural critic. I will say little about how women "really are in the world", or how they experience themselves and their dilemmas in relation to power. This is the purview of other contributors to this volume. I will, however, offer some thoughts about how women appear to men to struggle with the use of power and power relations. While I believe that my experience as a psychoanalyst has taught me a great deal about people—*men and women*—and about *life,* in truth we are all significantly limited by our own subjectivities, especially in such matters, more than we might like to or be able to acknowledge (psychoanalysts are making much of this epistemological humility these days). Therefore, in some immediate and intuitive ways, I probably know more about the male mind than the female mind, as I believe women know more about the female than the male mind. Beyond that, I must confess a sense (one shared by many psychoanalysts, evolutionary biologists, anthropologists, the media, and all women who have ever had a son or brother) that women may know men better than men know women and, at times and in certain ways, better than they know themselves. To many, men seem to be truly novice explorers in the world of women, especially about women and power.

Perhaps the most dramatic case in point, and a most interesting and important case, is that of Sigmund Freud, a man obsessed with and fascinated by power. Intriguingly, his entire project—to construct a theory of mind, its developmental vicissitudes and its treatment—can be viewed as an elaborate treatise on the nature and meanings of power in human life. Freud created a new lens on the human condition based significantly on what constituted and embodied power. However, the Viennese "conquistador" is himself an exemplar *par excellence* of my theses. First, that men have great difficulty understanding the nature of women and their power. Second, that his theories of female psychology and sexuality include, in major measure, more truths about male psychology than about female psychology. That Freud may have been afraid of women does not appear obvious from the historical record. He grew up, according to him, as an object of unalloyed adoration of a young and beautiful mother who invested him with a guiding and abiding sense of specialness. He loved women, especially smart, younger women who adored and idolized him. What we do know about his views of women, much more than about his relationships with women, is most significantly revealed in his theories about them. I suggest that they display how mystified he was by them and how, in his efforts to understand them, he offered us an example of how men cope with their unconscious anxieties about women: *men diminish and weaken women*. Freud built his theoretical system about women essentially on the following construct: a woman as having to struggle in life as an "*homme manqué*", a castrated man. A woman through this lens is man's passive, dependent, submissive, vulnerable biological and moral inferior. Thus, what Freud reveals in his magnificent failure—his essential theory of female psychology—is a male fantasy, a model drawing heavily on the social norms of his time, in which there is a devaluation, a castration of the powerful, to relieve the anxiety associated with the universal struggles with fear, envy, and dependence in response to woman's power.

While a comprehensive review of Freud on female psychology is beyond the scope of this chapter (an excellent review of the psychoanalytic literature of female psychology, Freud, and beyond is given by Schuker & Levinson, 1991), the following reflect the essence of his fundamental concepts of female psychology.

His mystification found its clearest expression as described by Jones (1955), quoting Freud:

> There is little doubt that Freud found the psychology of women more enigmatic than that of men. He said once to Marie Bonaparte: "The great question that has never been answered and which I have not yet been able to answer, despite my thirty years of research into the feminine soul, is 'what does a woman want?'" [p. 468]

In 1925, in "Some Psychical Consequences of the Anatomical Distinction between the Sexes", in what we might call Freud's theoretical "ground zero" on this question, he asserts: "After a woman has become aware of the wound to her narcissism [castration], she develops, like a scar, a sense of inferiority"(1925j, p. 253).

Falling to the succeeding generations of women analysts to offer the necessary critique and corrective of Freud's theories of women, Karen Horney, most notably, effectively took up the issue. In "The Dread of Women", Horney (1932), anticipating much of the now current discussion of self-organization and self-esteem, criticizes Freud's theories. She recognized that the dread of mother (woman) is much greater and deeper than the fear of the father. Castration anxiety is not a sufficient explanation of the dread of women in men. Reviewing male developmental history, she asserts that the dread of women is prior to and more profound than that of other men: "From all this I think it probable that the masculine dread of the woman (mother) or of the female genital is more deep seated, weighs more heavily and is usually more energetically repressed than the dread of the man (father)" (p. 352). "The boy's original dread of women is not castration anxiety at all but a reaction to the menace to his self respect" (p. 356). Concluding, she writes: "According to my experience the dread of being rejected and derided is a typical ingredient in the analysis of every man, no matter what his mentality or structure of his neurosis" (p. 357).

Finally, offering a bleak, and ultimately tragic view of the impact of this male problem on society, Horney envisions: "what really counts is the fact that the ever precarious self respect of the 'average man' causes him over and over again to choose a feminine type which is infantile, non-maternal and hysterical, and by so doing to expose each new generation to the influence of such women" (p. 360).

Following Horney, Ruth Moulton, in her paper "The Fear of Female Power: A Cause of Sexual Dysfunction" (1977), makes quite clear the dilemma that men face with women:

> Mother gives the first sensual gratification but is also the first to stop the flow of milk and of unconditional acceptance, to forbid sexual activities and impose restrictions, as in toilet training. Thus ambivalence toward mother seems unavoidable; yearning for and rage against mother's (woman's) body is clearly discernable in analysis and helps to explain many phenomena, such as fear of female retaliation, and displacement of dread and revulsion onto the female genitalia, the fear of sexuality inadequacy in the male. [p. 501]

Summing up, she states:

> The ambivalence about women is very clear, they can be deified and endowed with the attributes of abundance or transformed into figures of terror and menace. [p. 502]

Freud, as we see, in fundamental ways missed the boat about women and power, and a veritable intellectual industry has been built to ensure that this is not forgotten.

Widening the aperture of the psychoanalytic lens on the question of power, I suggest that analysts and analytic theorizing have developed various ways of describing, defining, and explaining power. Indeed, the various theoretical frames of references, the differing conceptualizations of psychological life, are slightly differing vocabularies for the nature and place of power in our inner mental lives and emotional development. Much discussion and debate today is focused on the compatibility and potential integration of the various perspectives. Nonetheless, one idea remains clear and unarguable. We, as human beings, dread and seek to avoid the experience of powerlessness. However defined or expressed, a sense of self, a core sense of agency as a conscious living creature, intrinsically includes a sense of autonomy, of power, and of capacity to effect events in the world, a sense of our ability to both predict and influence forces in our world; this is essential in our adaptation, for our safety and satisfaction. All our psychoanalytic concepts of motivation—of drives, object relational wishes and fears, self-organization, and self-esteem, and so forth—all motives are forms of power to assess and respond to the environment in which we develop and live. Therefore, power is a universal and ubiquitous concern to us every day. Life is experienced in the language of our power to know and to act.

There is another inescapable truth about power in our lives. Evolution has endowed us with and artfully sculpted in us a predetermined preoccupation with where we fit in in relation to our fellow humans, where we sit or stand in the group or horde. Whether we choose to comply or defy this evolutionary imperative, we are designedly hierarchical creatures. Certainly, we take pride in believing that our hierarchical concerns are more complex, more variegated, and more symbolic than our nearest primate relatives, in believing that we, as humans, are less in the thrall of this structuring of sociobiology. In our own terms, we are driven to know—whether we are consciously aware of it or not—where we are in the "pecking order" of submission and dominance in our lives. Almost everything we do or have carries some social ordering signifier of our place. In women and men, this force takes interesting and importantly differing forms of expression, forms of expression that involve status held and status sought in self and partner. It is unavoidable. As a consequence, our sense of self and of safety, our sense of satisfaction and contentment, is imbued with sometimes overt and sometimes covert indicators of where and how we fit in.

With this perspective on the centrality of power concerns in our core biological, psychological, and social priorities, what about men's perspective on women and power?

Men fear women, and with good reason! Women are power. Men, whatever they may say or do, stand in awe and dread of women. Women possess the obvious powers to create and define life and living. All children, including male children, are fascinated by and hungry to find themselves through, and to be defined by, their mothers. Mothers intuitively know this and define the child to the child and the child's place in and relationship to the world from the very beginning of life; in fact, the anticipated child of pregnancy is endowed with wished-for and feared qualities that will greet it on arrival. In current developmentalist parlance, this is what is meant by the concept of the self-reflective function and mentalization (Fonagy & Target, 1997a, 1997b) . The mind is created or at least profoundly sculpted in important ways in the maternal–infant dyad, the interactional/relational structuralization of the mind and brain. In this experience, we crave being looked at and heard (literally), being seen, being recognized, being envisioned. We become ourselves in the process of having attention paid to us. Without it we die, first in spirit and then in body. Our emerging emotional life depends upon this *attentional*, "including us", process. This process—what I have called "the woman as looking glass" for a man—continually evolves and grows in depth and complexity over time and subsumes all the well-marked developmental milestones: dependence, attachment, separation–individuation, self-definition, self-regulation, moral development, socialization, sexuality, intimacy, independence, ambition, ideals, and so forth along the entire arc of emotional development. All a man can want and need incorporates some sense of being looked upon as worthy; this is the fulcrum of healthy and unhealthy narcissism.

In this sense, women have the power and the burden, in significant measure, to make men of men and, perhaps more fundamentally, into relating human beings. Men may and often do grow up with a dialectical addiction to and aversion to being defined by women. This finds intricate and intensely conflictual forms of expression in the narcissistic psychopathology of men, about which more below.

Implicated in this defining relational power is the development of the early moral emotions. Nowhere is this more evident than in the organizing influence of the crucial social affects, pleasurable pride, overwhelming shame, and crushing guilt. These affective organizers of our emerging sense of self create the meanings of experience, particularly the experience of a self as having power, of becoming autonomous, and establishing self-worth. There is no subjective experience without emotional valence, and shame and guilt are crucial early moral affective forces.

Shame and guilt are compelling moral emotions; however, even and perhaps especially for the growing child, there is a profound and inescapable existential difference in the nature and meaning of shame and guilt. Guilt was the central moral force on which psychoanalytic theory and treatment was originally constructed by Freud and his immediate followers. Freud had remarkably little to say about shame. Its importance had to await the deepening appreciation of the nature of narcissism. For guilt, for Freud (and now the Lacanians) it is the voice of the father that becomes the voice of conscience, the persona of the superego. With guilt, there is crime and punishment. There is hope that it is in one's power to perform acts of contrition, of expiration, of restitution to repair or undo the transgression. Psychoanalysis was built on the foundation of punishment of castration. Oedipus' crime was great and his punishment was great. But there was at least something he could do to bring justice. Some wrongs can be righted.

Not so, however, with shame. If guilt is about doing wrong, shame is about being wrong, about being the wrong kind of being. When in the well of shame, there is no power for repair; there is only abject surrender to it. Shame, if you watch it in little children with their fallen faces and slumped bodies, is the experience of being the wrong kind of being and therefore excluded. It is the essential question: what is wrong about me? Not, what have I done wrong? Developmentally, shame involves global self attribution, not the specific attribution associated with guilty action.

Only the other, only mother (the "Ur" woman in all our lives) for this discussion, can repair this state of self. Only mother, the primary caregiver and self-definer, possesses the power to make us right again, to bring us back in, to look upon us and replace shame with joyful pride and self-worth. This underlying and overall sense of woman as possessing multidimensional power—that is, to create or destroy within a man the sense of being intact or whole, fake, or real, of being cared for, of being valued, desired and needed, of being a man—this power engenders in men the awe and dread that shapes and colours relationships with women generally in life. When women have real and objective power over men—for example, in vocational, professional, social, and financial situations—this dynamic is intensified. Often, it is what makes men more comfortable with other men in positions of power.

How do men cope with this awe and dread? Whether acknowledged or not, men can struggle with their envy and anxiety, their dependence and their desire, in adaptive and maladaptive, socially constructive and socially destructive ways.

Male spousal abuse has many determinants, certainly including alcoholism, drug abuse, and various forms of severe psychopathology. Furthermore, wives also abuse husbands, although much less frequently than husbands abuse wives. Men often mistreat and abuse women emotionally and physically when they fear, in real and imagined ways, the reflection of themselves offered back by the woman or women in their lives. When they fear weakness, inadequacy, and failure, they fear their obvious dependence on the woman. When they experience their larger world as frustrating, disappointing, ignoring, or humiliating them, they will strike out to defend themselves in some fashion. In more socially acceptable forms, men will seek women as expressions of or trophies symbolizing their power, sometimes as talismans against the dread of aging and the fear of their own mortality. When men experience real or imagined inflations and/or deflations in their sense of power, they may express it sexually.

Addressing this issue in her fascinating paper, "Male Sexuality and Power", Ethel Person (1993), explores male fantasies of sexual dominance, noting the defensive role that power fantasies play in warding off various narcissistic injuries experienced by men during development. Through power and submission, sexual fantasy and sexual play, these men can modulate turbulent internal affective states and control disintegrative anxieties. Person writes:

> When I say that the male resorts to power remedies, I use the term "power" not in the sense of a set of impulses to defeat competitors but in the sense of imbuing the penis with mastery and ensuring a source of gratification by supplying a fantasied plethora of lusty women over whom he is lord. [p. 35].

Another common manifestation of defence and repair, seen in clinical situations because of the marital upheaval it causes, is the emergence of a previously insecure man, a former "nerd", now grown up who in his forties or fifties acquires significant professional and/or financial power. What does this man do? He may leave the woman upon whom he has depended in his rise to power and fortune and seek out a younger, more apparently sexually appealing, woman, a woman who will ostensibly be in awe of his money and power. This new woman or new women are experienced by such a man as less powerful. But what he seeks, unconsciously, is to acquire for himself the power that these women symbolically represent in their sex, procreativity, youth, and beauty. This new woman or women will, so the wish goes, make a man of him once again, only better this time. Then, this man can face his adversaries and adversities renewed and emboldened.

Summarizing Freud and all of psychoanalysis most succinctly, Robert Michels (personal communication) wryly suggested: "Everything is about sex, except sex; sex is about power." To which he added: "Sometimes sex is just about sex!" While sexuality can be used and misused defensively to assert or claim power, the reverse is seen as well. Sexual desire and sexual gratification encounter the issue of power relations. From the male perspective—and certainly the theme in literature, endless good and bad jokes, and the advice that mothers and fathers gave to their daughters and sons—*women control access to sex*. Men want sex; sex serves a variety of unconscious needs in men—forms of anxiety relief, repair, object hunger. (Certainly this is true in women as well; men do not have an exclusive franchise on the healthy and neurotic uses and misuses of sex, though they are different.) For heterosexual men, women have the power to grant sexual access and sexual satisfaction. Women have used sex to gain power. Women are courted (in spite of today's rhetoric and the image of female sexual aggressiveness). Indeed, they have considerable influence and control over the nature of the pursuit; women have the power to be pursued or not, in general. Women grant sexual satisfaction to men and then have the considerable power to judge the man's performance, his adequacy; the price of sexual access can be self-esteem. Women learn early and well, generally (or at least they should), that men want sex and that men want to believe (in spite of their grave doubts) that they are actually good at it—good in bed. Women have the power to grant sex and relieve anxiety; they can deem the man adequate, crown him a success, or crush him as a failure.

How do men view women in the exercise of their (women's) power? In the psychology of men, the dangers associated with the exercise of power seem relatively straightforward. Men fear retaliation or failure most generally in the exercise of power. Men may wish to be liked in the exercise of their power. They are socialized, and trained, and encouraged to feel enhanced masculinity and self-esteem with the judicious use of power. And they fear being "feminized" when submitting to another man's power; just watch what can happen on the road if one man tries to cut in front of another—there can be fatal consequences.

Like beauty, power is in the eyes of the beholder. Since men must deal with their own fears of women, they may (and often do) view women as more ambivalent about power. Women seem to feel that much more is at stake in the position of power and more uneasy about the risks that come with power. The most obvious is how power "defeminizes" a woman: a woman may fear a loss of femininity and sexual appeal when in positions of power. I am not suggesting that this is indeed true of women as they experience themselves in positions of power, though it may be for some women. Clinically, masochistic adaptation by some women in power can take dramatic and tragic forms. Such women display profound neurotic inhibitions of their authentic abilities. The need to preserve an idealized male, the oedipal struggle to maintain a dependent relationship with an idealized father, may lead these women to deny and avoid appropriately challenging men. Fear of guilt that would come with defeating mothers and sisters, symbolically represented by female colleagues and peers, causes some women to defeat themselves or abandon ambitions for which they are most able. In "Women in the Maze of Power and Rage", Roy

Schafer (1993) incisively examines the meanings of victimization in the inner struggles of powerful and successful women. Often presenting themselves for analysis as victims trapped in rageful relations with difficult, insensitive, self-involved men, Schafer concentrates

> on two themes in the daughter–mother relationships I am describing, which seem to be two sides of the same coin. . . . The themes are damaged self-esteem regulation and unconscious ambivalent identification with the dominating and intrusive mother. [p. 23]

He summarizes:

> Here [reparation by the daughter of the crippled mother], love and guilt joined forces with rage, grandiosity, and humiliation to make these analysands victims who were simultaneously powerful forces in their own right. However much each one suffered in love and however abjectly she conducted herself outwardly in her heterosexual affairs and even in the workplace, she carried power and rage with her in the maze that was her life. [p. 26]

Indeed, when women are secure and clear in their power role, when they are not caught in the maze, men who themselves are not particularly burdened by their fear of women experience these women in power as better and more effective leaders and less confusing to men. When men have difficulties in their relationships with powerful women, when unconscious fears of women burden self-esteem and impulse control, such men tend to defensively regress to those rageful, distorted images of women as either desexualized and trying to be men, or as insatiable, devouring castrators and destroyers of men. In an effort to deal with a profound sense of threat, vulnerable men may overtly and inappropriately sexualize the work situation in an effort to regain "the upper hand", a restored sense of dominance and control. Consider male-dominance fantasy—the "James Bond" fantasy, the fantasy of overwhelmingly seductive phallic power that will triumph over feminine power. This fantasy rests in the presumed female "Achilles heel"—her need to be loved and need to be attractive, which is then expressed directly and indirectly in male forms of sexual harassment.

Returning to clinical considerations of the narcissistic psychopathology of men mentioned above, I suggest that it is useful at times to see in certain men the construct "woman as symptom", a typology in the heterosexual relationships of narcissistic men as they contend with profound fears of shame and powerlessness. What Freud got wrong in a most creative fashion was his emphasis on the damaged woman rather than on the damaging woman. Women are frightening not because they have been born damaged and therefore it is now possible for the male to experience the same fate. It is that women have enormous power and they can damage men if men get to close to them—versions of the "praying mantises in love" fantasy. Clinically, this is expressed in many forms in the narcissistic psychopathology of men: most obviously, those men who find it impossible to commit to a woman in an intimate and mutually interdependent relationship. Closeness brings with it multiple potential dangers: exposure of shameful and humiliating dependent wishes and needs; of fragile self-esteem and fears of inadequacy; of feared failure to meet the woman's imagined overwhelming demands; and, finally, of fear of the woman's searing, devastating rage. Once had, the woman must be turned into a devalued disappointment and left in order to avoid exposure of the man's own narcissistic vulnerabilities. In my experience, this is particularly true in the analyses of men who had absent, depressive and/or narcissistic mothers. Such men fear their own unmet dependency needs, and they deny and project them into the women with whom they attempt relationships, seeing the women as clingy and needy. Alternatively, they fear the intrusive control that is the legacy of the maternal relationship and inappropriately need to dominate the relationship in hurtful ways. Some men fear the devaluation and dominance that will follow the surrender to one woman, and so they must repeatedly conquer women to ward off their own self-hating sense of injury or emptiness. One man described only really feeling alive "in the chase". The sex itself ultimately was irrelevant at best, deadening at worst. The need to feel in control of the other reflected the underlying fear of being controlled. "Diversifying your investment" was how another man described it, explaining how he always had more than one woman in his life so as not to feel too dependent on any one woman. Unconsciously, his poorly integrated self-image depended terrifyingly on women to hold up a "mirror", to define him as he had felt defined by his mother as ideal, more a man than his weak father only as long as he never defied her. This man's rage and fear of women dominated his life. He came to treatment at around age 50 when he dreaded losing his potency. Another analysand had an intriguing reparative variation. He unconsciously hoped to find powerful fathers hidden in powerful women. He "desexualized" himself and hoped to be the irreplaceable ally and advisor to the "Queen". This led to inhibitions of assertion and ambition in his life and a quiet chronic uninterest in sex in his marriage. With treatment, he came to realize that his attempts to be a "royal eunuch" were driven by a wish to find a protector on whom he could depend in his fear of his rageful and capricious mother.

In conclusion, power concerns are integral in all human affairs. We are social creatures from birth, dependent on our caregivers to introduce us to ourselves and to the world. Men experience women with awe and dread because of this profound power, and men struggle to forge sound, integrated internal representations of themselves and of women in order to establish mature, realistic, and gratifying relationships in their lives. Questions remain when men look at women, questions attracting attention in education, in psychotherapy, in careers: do women feel their power and feel safely powerful only in a parallel universe, a world separate from men? Are women pretending to be threatened by men when they fear competition among themselves? Do women, in the eyes of men, have a falsely vulnerable and depreciated sense of themselves and of their awesome fundamental power?

CHAPTER TEN

Men's view of power in women: a woman's perspective

Helen Meyers

I find myself in a somewhat strange position as a woman involved in a discussion on *men's* view of power in women and of women in power. My data are thus indirect, from the analyses of men by women analysts—from my own practice and from suggestions and, more impressionistic, as the recipient of such male attitudes towards me (as a presumably "powerful" woman) from male colleagues and friends—as well as from observing hierarchies in our cultural institutions, political, social, and academic. You may have noticed that, inevitably, there is much overlap between the chapters, and this is good, since it suggests we all are on the right track. Stereotyped, *conscious* male views and reactions to *powerful women* have undergone a good deal of change from Victorian days and are still changing—a strong woman, for example, is no longer accused of "trying to be a man"—though changes in attitudes towards women in power have lagged behind changes in individual relationship attitudes. The *unconscious* determinants of views and reactions, on the other hand, I think have not really changed that much over time, being based on some early universal and individual dynamic and genetic factors in mother–child interactions, whose *individual* resolutions and compromises, however formed, vary widely between different men.

I differentiate between power in women and women in power. One refers to an internal integration of the self, to an internal sense of strength and power the other refers to a position of power, an external observable situation. "Strong" women do not necessarily attain positions of power, and women in power are not necessarily strong within themselves, may not experience themselves as strong, but may grow into such a self-identity. Some women have strength from their early upbringing, others develop it through much internal work and even adversity. Others have power thrust upon them. Inner struggle and power involve self-*assertion;* the attainment of power positions often involves *aggression.* How does a woman attain an inner sense of strength and power?

Among other things, this involves validation of the self by mother and/or father, identification with a strong father or mother, acceptance by the parent of the girl's strength and individuation, and competition without hostility. There are many different pathways for a woman to get to a position of power—pathways that I will discuss in more detail later—such as through aggressive competition, sadomasochistic manipulation, or erotic manipulation serving a "need for power"; or through nurturing and supporting others who become, in turn, devoted and supportive followers; or, of course, through genuine, recognized accomplishments. Or, of course, the position may not involve real, objective power but be only experienced as such in the eyes of the beholder—as the analyst is experienced by the analysand.

Men, of course, vary widely in their conscious and unconscious view and reaction to power and strength in women. Some men are completely comfortable with strong women—for various reasons, including security in their "masculinity"—others are not. It is common wisdom that each will differ depending on his background and development, parental empathy, support, and identification, his intrapsychic world, his dynamics and fantasy, and his own inner strength and view of himself. At the same time, however, some frequent common clusters of views and reactions may be found. Certainly, most men as little boys have mothers who were experienced preoedipally as the "giantesses of the nursery" and later as oedipal love objects. Though much of this is resolved in development and with parental empathy and appropriate support and nurture, some of these representations remain throughout life; depending on parental attitudes, mother–child interactions, life circumstances, conflicts and resulting compromises, these may manifest themselves in a variety of ways:

1. The "strong" women (or the female seen as strong) may be viewed by the man as controlling, demanding, extracting, castrating, ready to re-absorb the boy-man into her womb (which may be partially the boy's own desire) in an unconscious equation with the "bad" preoedipal mother image—to which danger the man may react with fear, avoidance, hatred, and attack; or, defensively, with put-down and denigration of the woman to lessen the image of her destructive power; or he may react with sadomasochistic submission and excitement.
2. Or the "strong" woman may continue to be equated unconsciously with the "good" preoedipal mother, viewed as protecting, giving, loving, caretaking—to which the man may react by seeking out the strong woman, with admiration, adoration, and love for meeting his needs of love and dependency. Of course, paradoxically this looking for the "good", "strong" mother may also be the result of a lack of fulfilment of these needs earlier, rather than the memories of fulfilment.
3. Or the envy and jealousy the little boy feels for the powerful mother and her procreative power may carry over into permanent envy of strong women, into a need to outdo them creatively in other areas and an attempt to tear them down.
4. Or the boy may have identified with the strength of the mother, and the man continues to look for a strong woman, sometimes viewed as the phallic female, in order to continue to support and solidify this joint strength.

This brings us to sex and power. The powerful woman, representing the big oedipal mother, is unconsciously viewed as exciting and forbidden, the object of desire, leading to guilt and avoidance, but also as the powerful woman who can both give and withhold sex and thus control the man. Remember Somerset Maugham's *Of Human Bondage*, where the woman almost destroys the man through his dependence on her sexually; remember the story of Lysistrata, where the women coerced the men into stopping the war by withholding sex; and remember history and Mrs Simpson (Wally), for whose sexual favours Edward VIII gave up his throne.

It gets more complicated than that, however. The strong woman viewed as potentially *castrating*, as mentioned before, is also viewed as *castrated* even though strong. This makes her doubly dangerous, because of her potentially castrating wish and power to take the penis away from the man to replace her lack and also because, in the man's wish to *identify* with her *strength*, he flirts with a castrated image of himself. The castrated image of the female may have to be desired unconsciously—such as in fetishism—or it may be used consciously defensively as a means of lessening the perceived power of the woman in the man's fantasy.

Sometimes one of the above clusters is dominant, frequently these may be a combination. Let me present two short clinical vignettes from analytic practice. These samples are somewhat skewed since the patients presented pathologic solutions and views of strong women yet also sought out women for therapists whom they viewed as powerful.

Patient I is a young, professional man with a background of an inadequate father and a dominating mother. Mother was seductive with the boy, belittling and denigrating of the father, and she carried on a long-standing affair, which she flaunted in front of the father and son. The patient felt betrayed, furious, as well as titillated as a boy and as a man. He consciously seemed to avoid powerful women, and he married a small, quiet submissive wife, consciously setting up a relationship where this would not happen again and he would be the boss. Curiously, however, he chose a woman as his analyst. He viewed his analyst as a powerful woman in a position of power over him, whom he could not trust and who would betray him as well as exploit him sexually and abuse him. At times he tried to turn the tables and belittle the analyst; at times he would act out hostility; at times he had strongly erotic dreams involving the analyst and, in general, submitted and attacked in a sadomasochistic transference. This all was most picturesquely demonstrated in a dream in which *the analyst was the female German concentration camp commander in a film, "Seven Beauties", who was a fat, sadistic woman who exploited her power to make the prisoner-hero submit to her sexually in a most humiliating way—a prisoner, however, who himself manipulatively sought her out in order to gain favours and service.* The fact that the analyst had a German accent and was heavy helped the use of this Nazi image, despite the fact that he knew she was Jewish, but it was primarily the patient's psychic representations of powerful women that created the image. This was a long and combative analytic encounter. Much later, when the patient began to get in touch with some warm and tender feelings in relation to mother, he was able to bring out his view of the analyst as potentially using her power *for* him, to protect and care for him—which was probably part of his unconscious fantasy why he chose a "powerful" female analyst in the first place.

Patient II presented himself as distressed over his inability to establish a permanent relationship with a woman. His father was considered a failure; his mother, aunts, and sister were viewed as powerful and critical, demolishing father but seductive with the boy (patient). The patient himself was well educated and successful, with many cultural and artistic interests and talents, but he could not enjoy his many activities when not involved with a woman. Time and again he would look for a powerful woman, "fall in love", establish an intense, mutually adoring relationship. After six or eight months, he would invariably find what to him seemed a major flaw in the woman—she had fat legs, she wanted children, she was critical—and he would abruptly break off the relationship, leaving the woman devastated and himself lonely and depressed. As expected, when his therapy with a woman reached eight months, he tried to abruptly terminate. It was only when this was explored, the pattern confirmed, that he began to be in touch with his view of strong women (like his mother) as desirable and fascinating, but also as controlling, critical, and destructive to men—women whom he felt he needed but also from whom he fled to save his life—and thus finally he got in touch with his intense rage at them, of which he had been completely unaware.

Male reactions to women in *power positions*—as differentiated from simply a strong woman—tend to be less varied, imbued with more cultural stereotypes in addition to their individual intrapsychic contributions. Many men tend to be vaguely threatened and uncomfortable with women in power positions. These women already *in* power are often seen as too tough and competitive. If not there already, strong and competent women often are not "heard" or thought of for leadership positions, being viewed defensively as potentially weaker, less able to act decisively, less imbued with a particular masculine intelligence and logic, more emotionally motivated and thus not to be trusted, possibly even dangerous. This may be changing, slowly, but, for example, in the United States there still is no seriously considered female candidate for the presidency (though there have been women leaders of state in other countries) and there still are relatively few women chairs of departments in our universities.

Now, how do women get to positions of power?

1. Our pathway involves straightforward aggressive and hostile competition, based on a "need for power" derived from early helplessness and powerlessness, in which scenario the oppressing competition is demolished and the man fearfully submits. An interesting subgroup of this, which works in personal relationships as well as political power play, is much more complex: as a little girl in search of love from father, she was deprived or was abused, but also learned to be seductive. As an adult women, in unconscious reactive anger, she projects this hostility onto the workers around her, expecting attack, and thus defensively first attacks and then demolishes the other. Once the other is fearfully demolished, some of her rage is abated and she is able to seductively embrace the other—both because she feels stronger in victory, but also she is now able to release some genuine, repressed, original need for "love". The other now intriguingly responds with admiration and adora-

tion, because he is relieved of the threat of being demolished, but also because he feels narcissistically elevated by being included in this power circle; but also he responds to the warmth and seduction. Men in such personal encounters often forget that they first felt threatened, hurt, and enraged and are only consciously aware of their admiration for this woman, her ability and charm, and then readily put her into a position of power.

In another subgroup of combined sex and aggression, the woman suppresses all aggression and, overtly using her sexuality, seduces the man into furthering her pursuit for power.

2. Another route to a position of power curiously does not primarily involve a "need for power" or hostility and aggression. Such a woman has a great capacity and wish to nurture, give, and support. This may be based on being the recipient of such nurture from her mother, or identification with an all-giving mother, or may be a compensation for an early lack of nurture. But, functioning in this supportive, mothering role towards all around her, a large cadre of grateful admirers collect who are not threatened by her but turn to her for advice, support, warmth, and validation and push her into a position of great influence and thus power—though not, perhaps, quite as powerful as the first group described above.
3. Finally, there is, of course, the woman who is simply highly gifted, talented, and accomplished, who quietly or enthusiastically goes about her work, whose very real achievements, respected by all, automatically put her into a position of eminence, leadership and thus power (Nobel Prize). This pathway is unrelated to a need for power, aggression, or competition on the part of the woman—though it may involve a demanding superego in the woman, which is not unrelated to internal competition and control.

Do men view these women differently, react differently to women according to how they got to power by these different pathways? I would like to think so, that logically they would see through the seduction to the underlying aggression, would be in touch with their own vulnerability for narcissistic or dependency supplies, would be able to judge objectively and appreciate genuine achievement. But it is hard to tell: first, because often women in power come along a combination of these pathways; second, because so much of every man's view is really determined by his own inner vision, inner fantasy, and intrapsychic reality, not by "objective" external reality.

REFERENCES

Alizade, A. M. (1993). La mujer y la sangre [Woman and blood]. *Revista de Psicoanisi, 50* (3): 527–533.

Alizade, A. M. (1995). *Clinica con la muerte* [Near death: clinical studies]. Buenos Aires: Amorrortu editores.

Alizade, A. M. (1999). *Feminine Sensuality*. London: Karnac.

Angier, N. (2000). For women in astronomy— a glass ceiling in the sky. *New York Times,* 15 February.

Applegarth, A. (1976). Some observations on work inhibitions in women. *Journal of the American Psychoanalytic Association, 24* (Suppl.): 251–269.

Baudelaire, C. (1981). *Fatal Destinies: The Edgar Poe Essays,* trans. J. F. Mele. Woodhaven, NY: Cross Country Press.

Beebe, B., & Lachman, F. M. (1988). The contribution of mother–infant mutual influence to the origins of self- and object representations. *Psychoanalytical. Psychology, 5*: 305–337.

Berscheid, E. (1999). The greening of relationship science. *American Psychologist, 54* (4): 260–266.

Bion, W. R. (1967). A theory of thinking. In: *Second Thoughts: Selected Papers on Psycho-Analysis.* London: Karnac.

Bowlby, J. (1980). *Attachment and Loss, Vol. 3: Loss, Sadness and Depression.* London: Penguin.

Buntman, F. (1995). Interview with Shawn Slovo, 6 March. In: I. Suttner (Ed.), *Cutting through the Mountain: Interviews with South African Jewish Activists.* New York: Viking, 1997.

Cavell, M. (1993). *The Psychoanalytic Mind: From Freud to Philosophy*. Cambridge, MA: Harvard University Press.

Chamberlain, D. (1987). The cognitive newborn: a scientific update. *British Journal of Psychotherapy 4*: 30–69

Chodorow, N. J. (1986a). Histoire et vie des premières femmes psychanalystes. *Psychothérapies, 6*.

Chodorow, N. J. (1986b). Varieties of leadership among early women psychoanalysts. In: L. Dickstein & C. Nadelson (Eds.), *Women Physicians in Leadership Roles*. Washington, D.C.: American Psychiatric Press.

Chodorow, N. J. (1987). Der Beitrag der Frauen zur Psychoanalytischen Bewegung und Theorie. *Psyche: Zeitschrift für Psychoanalyse und Ihre Anwendungen, 41*.

Chodorow, N. J. (1989). Seventies questions for thirties women: gender and generation in a study of early women psychoanalysts. In: *Feminism and Psychoanalytic Theory* (pp. 199–218). New Haven, CT: Yale University Press.

Chodorow, N. J. (1991). Where have all the eminent women psychoanalysts gone? Like the bubbles in champagne, they rose to the top and disappeared. In: J. Blau & N. Goodman (Eds.), *Social Roles and Social Institutions*. Boulder, CO: Westview Press (second edition, 1995).

Chodorow, N. J. (1999a). *The Power of Feelings*. New Haven, CT: Yale University Press.

Chodorow, N. J. (1999b). La psychanalyse et les femmes psychanalystes. In: S. de Mijolla-Mellor (Ed.), *Les femmes dans l'histoire de la psychanalyse*. Paris: L'Esprit du Temps.

Compton, A. (1985). Identification in Freud, Ferenczi and Abraham. *Psychoanalytic Quarterly, 54*: 201–233.

Clyman, R. (1991). The procedural organization of emotions: a contribution from cognitive science to the psychoanalytic theory of therapeutic action. *Journal of the American Psychoanalytical Association, 39*: 349–382.

De Casper, A. J., et al. (1987). Fetal perception and discrimination of speech stimuli: demonstrated by cardiac reactivity, preliminary results. *Compte Rendu de L'Academie des Sciences, 3* (30): 161–164.

Derrida, J. (1994). Roundtable discussion. Inauguration of Villanova University, 4 October.

Dinnerstein, D. (1976). *The Mermaid and the Minotaur: Sexual Arrangements and the Human Malaise*. New York: Harper & Row.

Dionne, E. J. (1999). Two for glory. *Washington Post*, 10 December, p. A47.

Dossey, L. (1999). *Reinventing Medicine: Beyond Mind-Body Medicine to a New Era of Healing*. San Francisco, CA: Harper.

Eliot, T. S. (1933). *The Use of Poetry and the Use of Criticism: Studies in the Relation of Criticism to Poetry in England*. London: Faber & Faber.

Ellmann, R. (1987). *Oscar Wilde*. London: Hamish Hamilton.
Emde, R. N. (1989). The infant's relationship experience: developmental and affective aspects. In: A. J. Samaroff & R. N. Emde (Eds.), *Relationship Disturbances in Early Childhood*). New York: Basic Books.
Erikson, E. H. (1950). *Childhood and Society*. New York: W. W. Norton.
First, R. (1965). *117 Days*. London: Penguin.
Fonagy, P. (1995). Playing with reality: the development of psychic reality and its malfunction in borderline personalities, *International Journal of Psycho-Analysis, 76*: 39–44.
Fonagy, P. (1999). Memory and therapeutic action. *International Journal of Psycho-Analysis, 80*: 215–223.
Fonagy, P., & Target, M. (1997a). Mentalization and the changing aims of child psychoanalysis. *Psychoanalytic Dialogues, 8* (1): 87–114.
Fonagy, P., & Target, M. (1997b). Attachment and reflective function: their role in self-organization. *Development and Psychopathology, 9* (4): 679–700.
Foucault, M. (1976). *Historia de la sexualidad*. Mexico: Siglo XXI editores, 1985.
Frank, H. (1977). Dynamic patterns for failure in college students. *Canadian Psychiatric Association Journal, 22*: 295–299.
Frankel, G. (1999). *Rivonia's Children*. New York: Farrar, Straus, & Giroux.
Freud, A. (1936). *The Ego and the Mechanisms of Defence*. London: Hogarth, 1976.
Freud, S. (1905e [1901]). Fragment of an analysis of a case of hysteria. *S.E., 7*.
Freud, S. (1909c). Family romances. *S.E., 9*.
Freud, S. (1910c). *Leonardo da Vinci and a Memory of His Childhood. S.E., 11*.
Freud, S. (1914c). On narcissism: an introduction. *S.E., 14*.
Freud, S. (1915). Nosotros y la muerte. Conference given in February 1915 at the Wien society, branch of the B´nai B´rith. *Revista de Psicoanàlisis, 68* (4, 1991): 677–687.
Freud, S. (1916d). Some character-types met with in psycho-analytic work. Those wrecked by success. *S.E., 14*.
Freud, S. (1919h). The "uncanny". *S.E., 17*.
Freud, S. (1923a [1922]). Two encyclopaedia articles.. *S.E., 18*.
Freud, S. (1923b). *The Ego and the Id. S.E., 19*.
Freud, S. (1924d). The dissolution of the Oedipus complex. *S.E., 19*.
Freud, S. (1925j). Some psychical consequences of the anatomical distinction between the sexes. *S.E., 19*.
Freud, S. (1927c). *The Future of an Illusion. S.E., 21*.
Freud, S. (1930a). *Civilization and Its Discontents. S.E., 21*.
Freud, S. (1931a). Libidinal types. *S.E., 21*.
Freud, S. (1936a). A disturbance of memory on the Acropolis. *S.E., 22*.

Freud, S. (1937c). Analysis terminable and interminable. *S.E., 23.*

Freud, S. (1939a [1937–39]). *Moses and Monotheism. S.E., 23.*

Freud, S. (1940a [1938]). *An Outline of Psycho-Analysis. S.E., 23.*

Freud, S. (1950 [1892–1899]). Extracts from the Fliess papers. *S.E., 1.*

Freud, S. (1950 [1895]). A project for a scientific psychology. *S.E., 1.*

Galenson, E., & Roiphe, H. (1976). Some suggested revisions concerning early female development. *Journal of American Psychoanalytic Association, 24* (Suppl., No. 5): 29–57.

Gassmann, V. (1996). Interview. *Clarin Journal* (Buenos Aires), 27 July.

Gay, P. (1984). The bourgeois experience: Victoria to Freud. In: *Education of the Senses.* London: Oxford University Press.

Gilligan, C. (1982). *In a Different Voice.* Cambridge, MA: Harvard University Press.

Gordimer, N. (1979). *Burger's Daughter.* Harmondsworth, Middlesex: Penguin.

Goudge, E. (Ed.) (1964). *A Book of Comfort.* New York: Coward-McCann.

Green, A. (1986). The dead mother. In: *On Private Madness.* London: Hogarth Press.

Harman, W. (1998). *Global Mind Change: The Promise of the 21st Century.* San Francisco, CA: Berrett-Koehler.

Harris, A. (1997). Aggression, envy, and ambition: circulating tensions in women's psychic life. *Gender & Psychoanalysis, 2*: 291–325.

Hopkins, N. (1999a). Editorial. *New York Times,* 12 July.

Hopkins, N. (1999b). A study on the status of women faculty in science at MIT. *MIT Faculty Newsletter 11* (4).

Horney, K. (1932). The dread of women. *International Journal of Psycho-Analysis, 13*: 348–360.

Horney, K. (1936). The problem of the negative therapeutic reaction. *Psychoanalalytic Quarterly, 5*: 29–44.

Hrdy, S. B. (1999). *Mother Nature: Natural Selection and the Female of the Species.* London: Chatto & Windus.

Hunter, S. (1999). "Joan" of burning confusion. *Washington Post,* 12 November, p. C5.

Janeway, E. (1971). *Between Myth and Morning: Women Awakening.* New York: William Morrow.

Jones, B. P. (1993). Repression: the evolution of a psychoanalytic concept from the 1890's to the 1990's. *Journal of the American Psychoanalytical Association, 41*: 63–94.

Jones, E. (1955). *Sigmund Freud: Life and Work, Vol. 2,* London/New York: Basic Books.

Keller, E. (1983). A *Feeling for the Organism: The Life and Work of Barbara McClintock.* New York: W. H. Freeman.

Kincaid, J. (1986). *Annie John.* New York: Penguin.

Koestler, A. (1964). *The Act of Creation.* London: Hutchinson.

Laplanche, J. (1995). Seduction, persecution, revelation. *International Journal of Psycho-Analysis, 76*: 663–682.

Levy, S., Seelig, B., & Inderbitzin, L. (1995). On those wrecked by success: a clinical inquiry. *Psychoanalytic Quarterly, 64*: 639–657.

Lipman-Blumen, J. (1996). *The Connective Edge: Leading in an Interdependent World*. New York: Jossey-Bass.

Marcus, E. (1999). Modern ego psychology. *Journal of American Psychoanalytical Association, 47*: 843–872.

Mathis, P. (1974). Etica y sexuación. In: *Actas de la Escuela Freudiana de París. VII Congreso de Roma*. Barcelona: Ediciones Petrel.

Mayer, E. L. (2000). Psychodynamic therapy: heading in new directions. In: J. Shay & J. Wheelis (Eds.), *Odysseys in Psychotherapy*. New York: Ardent Media.

Moulton, R. (1977). The fear of female power: a cause of sexual dysfunction. *Journal of the American Academy of Psychoanalysis, 5* (4): 499–519.

Moulton, R. (1986). Professional success: a conflict for women. In: J. L. Alpert (Ed.), *Psychoanalysis and Women*. Hillsdale, NJ: Analytic Press.

Murray, L., & Cooper, P. J. (1996). The impact of postpartum depression on child development, *International Review of Psychiatry, 8*: 55–63.

Netherlands Institute for War Documentation (1989). *The Diary of Anne Frank: The Critical Edition*, ed. D. Barnouw & G. van der Stroom; trans. Arnold J. Pomerans & B. M. Mooyaart. New York: Doubleday.

Nonnemaker, L. (2000). Women physicians in academic medicine. *New England Journal of Medicine, 342*: 399–405.

Parens, H. (1990). On the girl's psychosexual development: reconsideration suggested from direct observation. *Journal of the American Psychoanalytical Association, 38* (3): 743–772.

Parens, H. (1991). A view of the development of hostility in early life. *Journal of American Psychoanalytical Association, 39S*: 75–108.

Person, E. (1993). Male sexuality and power. In: R. Glick & S. Roose (Eds.), *Rage, Power, and Aggression*. New Haven, CT: Yale University Press.

Pert, C. (1997). *Molecules of Emotion*. New York: Simon & Schuster.

Pétrement, S. (1976). *Simone Weil: A Life*, trans. R. Rosenthal. New York: Pantheon Books.

Raphael-Leff, J. (1986). Facilitators and regulators: conscious and unconscious processes in pregnancy and early motherhood. *British Journal of Medical Psychology, 59*: 43–55.

Raphael-Leff, J. (1993). *Pregnancy: The Inside Story*. London: Sheldon Press.

Raphael-Leff, J. (1997a). Procreative process, placental paradigm and perinatal psychotherapy. *Journal of the American Psychoanalytic Association, 44* (Female Psychology Suppl.): 373–399.

Raphael-Leff, J. (1997b). The casket and the key: thoughts on gender and generativity. In: J. Raphael-Leff & R. Jozef Perelberg (Eds.), *Female Experience: Three Generations of British Female Psychoanalysts on Work with Women*. London/New York: Routledge.

Raphael-Leff, J. (2000). "Climbing the walls": puerperal disturbance and perinatal therapy. In: *Spilt Milk: Perinatal Breakdown and Loss*. London: Institute of Psychoanalysis.

Rimm, S., Rimm-Kaufman, S., & Rimm, H. (1999). *See Jane Win*. New York: Crown Publishers.

Riviere, J. (1929). Womanliness as a masquerade. In: *The Inner World and Joan Riviere: Collected Papers 1920–1958*. London: Karnac.

Rumi, M. J. (1998). *The Love Poems of Rumi*, ed. Deepak Chopra. New York: Harmony Books.

Sander, L. (1977). The regulation of exchange in the infant-caretaker system and some aspects of the context-content relationship. In: M. Lewis & L. Rosenblum (Eds.), *Interaction, Conversation and the Development of Language*. New York: Wiley.

Sandler, J. (1985) (with Freud, A.). *The Analysis of Defence: The Ego and the Mechanisms of Defence Revisited*. New York: International Universities Press.

Sandler, J. (1990). On internal object relations. *Journal of the American Psychoanalytical Association, 38*: 859–880.

Schafer, R. (1984). The pursuit of failure and the idealization of unhappiness. *American Psychologist, 39*: 398–405.

Schafer, R. (1993). Women in the maze of power and rage. In: R. Glick & S. Roose (Eds.), *Rage, Power, and Aggression*. New Haven, CT: Yale University Press.

Schuker, E. & Levinson, N. (1991). *Female Psychology: An Annotated Psychoanalytic Bibliography*. Hillsdale, NJ: Analytic Press.

Skolimowski, H. (1994). *The Participatory Mind: A New Theory of Knowledge and of the Universe*. London: Penguin.

Spitz, E. H. (1991). Mothers and daughters. In: *Image and Insight: Essays in Psychoanalysis and the Arts*. New York: Columbia University Press.

Stein, G. (1937). *Everybody's Autobiography*. New York: Random House.

Stein, G. (1973). *How to Write*. Barton, VT: Something Else Press.

Stein, G. (1990). *The Autobiography of Alice B. Toklas*. New York: Vintage Books.

Stein, G. (1998). Composition as explanation. In: *Gertrude Stein: Writings 1903–1932*, ed. C. R. Stimpson & H. Chessman. New York: Library of America.

Stein, R. (1998). The enigmatic dimensions of sexual experience: the "otherness" of sexuality and primal seduction. *Psychoanalytic Quarterly, 67*: 594–625.

Stern, D. (1985). *The Interpersonal World of the Infant: A View from Psychoanalysis and Developmental Psychology*, New York: Basic Books.

Szekely, L. (1960). Success, success neurosis and the self. *British Journal of Medical Psychology*, *33*: 45–51.

Trevarthen, C. (1980). The foundations of intersubjectivity: development of interpersonal and cooperative understanding in infants. In: D. Olson (Ed.), *The Social Foundations of Language and Thought: Essays in Honour of J. S. Bruner*. New York: W. W. Norton.

Weil, S. (1977). Spiritual autobiography. In: *The Simone Weil Reader*, ed. G. Panichas. Mt. Kisco, NY: Moyer Bell.

Wheatley, M. (1994). *Leadership and the New Science: Learning about Organization from an Orderly Universe*. San Francisco, CA: Berrett-Koehler.

Wheeler, J. A. (1974). The universe as home for Man. *The American Scientist*, November/December.

Williams, C. (1989). *Gender Differences at Work: Women and Men in Nontraditional Occupations*. Berkeley, CA: University of California Press.

Williams, C. (1992). The glass escalator: hidden advantages for men in the "female" professions. *Social Problems*, *39*: 253–267.

Williams, C. (1995). *Still a Man's World: Men Who Do "Women's Work"*. Berkeley, CA: University of California Press.

Williams, J. (2000). *Unbending Gender: Why Family and Work Conflict and What to Do about It*. New York: Oxford University Press.

Winnicott, D. W. (1947). Hate in the countertransference. In: *Through Paediatrics to Psychoanalysis*. London: Hogarth Press, 1975.

Winnicott, D. W. (1960). Ego distortion in terms of true and false self. In: *Maturational Processes and the Facilitating Environment*. New York: International Universities Press, 1965.

Winnicott, D. W. (1969). Development of the theme of the mother's unconscious ambivalence as discovered in psycho-analytic practice. In: *Psycho-Analytic Explorations*, ed. C. Winnicott, R. Shepherd, & M. Davis. London: Karnac; Cambridge, MA: Harvard University Press, 1989.

Winnicott, D. W. (1971). Mirror-role of mother and family in child development. In: *Playing and Reality*. New York: Basic Books.

Yourcenar, M. (1976). *The Abyss*, trans. G. Frick in collaboration with author. New York: Farrar Straus Giroux.

Yourcenar, M. (1984a). *With Open Eyes: Conversations with Matthieu Galey*, trans. A. Goldhammer. Boston, MA: Beacon Press.

Yourcenar, M. (1984b). *Alexis*, trans. W. Kaiser in collaboration with author. New York: Farrar Straus Giroux.

INDEX